HITOSHI ABE

Introduction

In March 2007 Hitoshi Abe boarded a plane bound for Los Angeles. Trading his hometown Sendai, a city of one million located 350 km (217 miles) north-east of Tokyo, for a new one in California, he was on his way to assume the Chair of the Department of Architecture & Urban Design at UCLA. Though born and brought up in Miyagi Prefecture, Abe was no stranger to California, having graduated from SCI-Arc and then working locally for several years, until a stunning victory in a football stadium competition forced his unexpected move back to Sendai. Building his practice in a regional Japanese city may not have been in Abe's original script. But serendipity worked in his favour. Here was the immediate chance to test out his ideas and build big – a very unusual opportunity for any newly trained, thirty-something designer. Bracketed between stays in Los Angeles, Abe's Sendai stint proved to be the defining period of his career to date. It was a prolific time, when he realized over 44 projects country-wide and emerged as a leading voice for his generation. Divided into three categories – Line, Surface and Volume – this body of work is the subject of this book.

What makes Abe worthy of attention is not just his dramatic debut. Nor is it only his cultural ambidexterity that makes his ideas accessible to audiences on both sides of the Pacific. It is his compelling architecture, whose elegant, and often dynamic, forms are the fruits of his rigorous, self-styled design process. To Abe, a preconceived functional or formal building typology may be a reasonable starting point. Yet so is any other model or shape. For construction convenience he uses standard Japanese measurements generated by tatami-mat dimensions. But conceptually he does not subscribe to any overriding organizational paradigm or coordinate system that exists independent of his buildings.

For Abe, design begins with an abstract geometric model such as a simple triangle, a sheet of steel, a ribbon of cardboard, an arched contour line, or a bubble-shaped volume. 'It doesn't really matter where you start,' says Abe. Devoid of meaning, these models are simply the medium for translating project particulars – topography, setbacks, building codes, material properties and client requests – into built form. As Abe explains, 'It is like clothing that's made of fabric and has its own structure but needs contact with the human body to define its shape.'

One of Abe's first trials using this approach arose in 1997 when he was asked to design an architectural installation for the courtyard of the Miyagi Museum of Art in Sendai. He decided to transform the landscape of the courtyard itself into a sculptural object that visitors could walk through. This required making precise measurements of the garden and its topography. Then, with the help of

Land Pack, Sendai, Miyagi Prefecture, 1997

computer software, Abe flipped his model ground plane over and adjusted the dimensions of its contours to fix the size of his finished object. The result was Land Pack: a three-dimensional grid made by Abe's students from wood planks left over from forest thinning nearby. Measuring 25 x 15 x 4.5 m (82 x 49 x 15 ft), the piece was architectural in scale but behaved like a free-standing work of art. Inspired by this outcome, Abe adapted the technique and used contour lines to derive the form of the Yomiuri Media Miyagi Guest House from its sloping, wooded site.

Instead of creating works that respond to project criteria, Abe uses these potentially limiting factors as his design tools. By allowing these conditions to modify, or even deform, his idealized, pristine shapes, Abe makes the abstract physically manifest. 'The final shape should talk about where it came from,' explains Abe. This approach stimulates invention and yields remarkably logical yet imaginative results that are very deeply rooted in their surroundings.

Unencumbered by external ordering devices, Abe's design method is very well suited to the broader context of Japan, where buildings tend to exist as isolated vignettes instead of as urban components. Distinguished by their unexpected shapes or unprecedented exterior enclosure, Abe's buildings take full advantage of the country's healthy appetite for architectural experimentation. In Japan, where contextual cues are minimal and zoning codes can be very forgiving, stylistic compatibility and shared aesthetics are dispensable commodities when it comes to new construction. And not just in Tokyo. Even in central Sendai, convenience stores and petrol stations stand side-by-side with Modernist office buildings on the city's gracious, tree-lined boulevards.

The visual cacophony of urban Japan is paralleled by the country's rich architectural history, with its common language of timber-frame construction, spare interiors and integration of the outdoors. Raised in and around Sendai, where he was far from the development frenzy that took hold of Tokyo in the 1960s, Abe had the chance to experience traditional buildings at first hand. 'The *engawa* space, a wide, wood-floored porch connecting different rooms and facing the garden, was where I played a lot,' Abe says of his childhood home. Though growing up in traditional-style timber houses left an indelible mark on Abe, his interest in architecture did not really coalesce until he entered the Department of Architecture during his undergraduate days at Tohoku University.

As a college student, Abe investigated buildings by Le Corbusier, Frank Lloyd Wright and other well-known Western architects. But, as in most Japanese universities, the architecture department fell under the aegis of the School of Engineering, and exposure to practising

Coop Himmelb(l)au, Folie for Osaka EXPO, Osaka, Osaka Prefecture, 1990

designers was negligible. For Abe this was a serious shortcoming. Though his academic studies enabled him to look closely at temples, shrines, farmhouses and other traditional buildings throughout Tohoku, the agricultural region surrounding Sendai, he realized early on that he would have to look elsewhere for design mentoring.

'My quest was "where do forms come from" and "how can we be sure which is the right one",' says Abe. At the time he did not know much about the United States, let alone architectural education abroad. In fact, he barely spoke English. But a brief encounter with the US-educated architects Shigeru Ban and Yoko Kinoshita convinced him to apply to overseas schools. 'It seemed like something was happening at SCI-Arc at the time,' says Abe. 'And given Los Angeles' proximity to Japan it seemed like a good place to live.'

Upon arriving in California, Abe was immediately impressed by his fellow students' zeal for their studies and the easy access to the star-studded cast of designers who lectured routinely on campus. An encounter with Peter Eisenman, who asserted that forms can come from outside architecture, even from the structure of DNA, opened Abe's eyes to a new way of thinking about design.

But a presentation by the Coop Himmelb(l)au principal Wolf Prix was the real turning point. As if tackling his question head on, Prix explained that a sketch made with his eyes closed generated the schematic design for his Open House project. From Prix's description Abe came to the conclusion that 'it doesn't really matter where design starts – there is no big difference between [using] a sketch done with your eyes closed or a mathematical model.'

Working in the Viennese architect's Los Angeles office, first as a student and then as a full-time employee after graduating from SCI-Arc in 1989, gave Abe the chance to absorb Prix's ideas and see them put into practice. At the time, the firm particularly welcomed Abe's input as they were one of seven foreign architects working on a folly project for the International Garden and Greenery Exhibition held in Osaka in 1990. Though it yielded only a temporary structure all but devoid of function, the project, a two-legged lookout tower made of steel, was a valuable professional experience that included translating sketch models into detailed drawings and liaising with the local architect in Japan.

But this training came to a sudden halt in 1992 when Abe decided to take a break from the office and go back to Sendai for a couple of months to welcome the arrival of his first child. Eager to continue working, he teamed up with local architect Shoichi Haryu and entered the competition for a new football stadium for the 2002 World Cup to be hosted jointly by Japan and Korea. With competition entries coming from world-famous architects

Miyagi Stadium, Rifu, Miyagi Prefecture, 2000, main stand

and the design departments of major construction companies, it seemed unlikely that a 30-year-old novice could win. But he did. Faced with this spectacular victory Abe could not possibly get back on the plane to California. He had no choice but to set up shop in Sendai and see the project through to completion.

Though staying put in Japan was a laboured decision for Abe, once he made up his mind he discovered a multitude of opportunities available to him back home. Unsurprisingly this high-profile project led to other commissions, first in collaboration with Haryu and then independently after founding his office, Atelier Hitoshi Abe, in 1993. Because of the paucity of design-oriented architects in the region – and even fewer with the caché of a degree from a foreign graduate school – Abe became the proverbial big fish in a small pond. 'In Sendai it is easier for clients to find you,' explains Abe. And, conversely, in a smaller arena it is easier for designers to access clients, even powerful bureaucrats and local business leaders.

While the chance to realize buildings may have motivated Abe's move, he returned to Sendai with a broader vision. 'In Japan you must be in Tokyo to do something interesting, but I wanted to stimulate growth here and transform Sendai into a hub of architectural culture,' explains the architect. He hoped that the attention garnered by his projects would elevate the status of the city and, ultimately, impact Japan's architectural scene as a whole.

Up until recently, Japan's regional cities were perceived as architectural backwaters, with the vast majority of design-oriented architects concentrated in Tokyo and, to a lesser extent, a couple of other big cities like Osaka. Typically, architects from Tokyo were parachuted in to design buildings out in the provinces. In some ways this trend raised design quality locally since it enabled some of the country's best designers to bring their fresh ideas even to remote parts of the country.

The downside of this system was the inherent risk that architects were designing for places they did not fully understand. 'They tended to look at the site from a bird's eye view,' according to Abe. As far as Tohoku was concerned, Abe could set this straight by living and working in Sendai. 'If you live in the countryside you get to know the fine points of the context,' says Abe. 'And that kind of closeness influences design.'

Practising what he preached, the designer opened his atelier in a modest, tiled-roof house in a residential neighbourhood. As the firm grew and its needs changed, Abe's team ripped out walls, expanded rooms and extended into a neighbouring house. But eventually a request from the wholesale distributors' union to analyse the future growth possibilities of Oroshimachi, the city's 55 hectare (138 acre) union-controlled warehouse district, prompted a full-scale office move. Instead of commenting

Oroshimachi warehouse district, Sendai, Miyagi Prefecture, 2006

← Miyagi Stadium, Rifu, Miyagi Prefecture, 2000, main stand, supporting structure

from a distance, Abe decided to relocate – a pioneering act that enabled him to observe neighbourhood activity at close range, become acquainted with its users and catalyse change from within.

Located on Sendai's comparatively undeveloped east side, the district is conveniently close to the city's commercial centre and its bullet-train station, but it was historically closed to tenants outside the goods distribution business. Though it is still in active use, changes in Japan's distribution network have impacted activity in the area to some extent. 'It is a kind of hole within the fabric of the city centre,' explains Abe. Aside from the occasional convenience store or fast-food outlet it is all but devoid of shopping, restaurants and other amenities. Instead, cavernous storage facilities, all still controlled and used almost exclusively by members of the delivery workers' union, comprise each block. Organized by a web of wide streets intended for trucks, the district interior is light-filled and shadow-free, yet trees are few and pedestrians are nowhere in sight.

'In a way it was a challenge to move here,' says Abe. But the architect saw the potential of this infrastructure and the large but mostly low-scale buildings with their loft-like interiors. Instead of trying to whitewash it with a visionary master plan, Abe's 'domestic urbanism' approach was to modify the neighbourhood gradually, stimulating new activities and making a series of modest adjustments to its physical layout from within. When the union offered him a 10-year lease on a former fabric warehouse in the heart of the neighbourhood, Abe could not pass up the vast, airy volume with plenty of space for models, material samples and the other detritus that often accumulates in architects' offices. In 2002 Abe's atelier moved to the newly retro-fitted storage shed that they affectionately named 'House' and still call 'home' today.

Turning the uninhabited industrial space into a user-friendly 297 m^2 (3,197 sq ft) architectural office took some doing. In addition to partitioning off a conference room, kitchen and lavatory, the architects added a space-defining mezzanine made of painted black wood – an element borrowed from the antique rice storehouse that Abe transformed into the Michinoku Folklore Museum. The majority of the building is an open, double-height space divided by clusters of desks belonging to Abe and his eight-person team. Convenient for model-making, magazine display and the occasional meal, a long steel counter dominates the centre of the room. While the warehouse's rolling garage door is an asset in summer, when the staff can practically peel away an entire wall, added insulation and flooring barely keep the high-ceilinged space comfortable in winter. As is the preferred practice in most of Japan, the chilly architects offset the low temperatures with hot drinks and portable heaters.

Atelier Hitoshi Abe, Sendai, Miyagi Prefecture, 2002, facade (top), studio (bottom)

Another way Abe has brought architectural prominence to Sendai is through the classroom. After returning from Los Angeles he received his PhD from Tohoku University in 1993 and then began teaching at Tohoku Institute of Technology. In 2002 he returned to his Alma Mater and at 40 years of age became one of Tohoku University's youngest full professors of architecture ever. During his tenure Abe focused his efforts on raising the quality of design education university-wide by mentoring the undergraduate and graduate students under the aegis of his research laboratory and in the capacity of the Director of the Architectural Design Education Committee. Keen to reduce the isolation from Japan's leading architects that he remembered from his own student days, Abe brought strong designers from Tokyo and other parts of Japan to lecture and teach at his university. And by setting up workshops and exchange programmes with architecture schools in Europe and the United States, he was able to bridge the international gap as well.

But Abe's contribution to the nation's architectural discourse is not confined to Tohoku University's hill-top campus. To spread the transmission of ideas and encourage dialogue among designers, he converts his office into a 150-seat lecture hall several times a year and invites designers to come and speak. And to draw attention to future architects nation-wide, he initiated the Number One Thesis competition in 2003. Following the model of the immensely popular National High School Baseball Tournament held annually near Kobe, architects come from all over Japan to judge the competition intended to select the single best undergraduate architectural design thesis each year. Held at Sendai Mediatheque, Toyo Ito's inspirational mixed-media centre just minutes from Abe's office, this two-day public forum singles out the country's most promising designer from among 500 entrants and shines a spotlight on Sendai at the same time.

The enthusiasm for the Number One Thesis competition in part reflects Japan's current architectural climate. Changes in architectural training and the distribution of information have made the awarding of commissions considerably more merit-based. In the 1960s and 1970s Japan's leading designers were educated at a handful of prestigious universities, mostly in Tokyo, and then underwent years of practical training in established firms. Commissions were often handed down from mentor to protégé or attained through social connections. As a result, the bulk of important design jobs were realized by a fairly limited number of architects, and very few successful designers developed practices outside this system. Tadao Ando, and years later Shigeru Ban, were the most visible exceptions.

This system was forced open in the 1980s when Japan's economic 'Bubble' period spawned a seemingly unlimited supply of design work and gave globalization a big push. In response, architects from all over the world flocked to Japan in search of work. And domestically the robust economy convinced many young designers to skip the arduous apprenticeships and launch practices of their own instead. Though this boom gave rise to buildings of varying quality, it heightened design awareness throughout the country.

As contact with the rest of the world increased, travel and architectural education outside Japan became more commonplace and the cross-fertilization of ideas proliferated. The surging propagation of information through architectural publications and the ever-growing use of the Internet compounded this international exchange. Within Japan these developments directly impacted architectural practice, since the combination of media access and easy communication enabled clients to search out and contact designers directly. Once the old system changed there was no going back. Even after the money dried up.

As a result of these events the Japanese architecture world today is far more accepting of different approaches to design training, construction and aesthetics. Because of this broadening Abe is not exactly an outsider. But he is not entirely an insider either. According to Abe this is due in part to his geographic location. 'I never went to Tokyo,' says the Sendai native. 'This is a big, big difference in my background.' But Abe's ambiguous relationship to his peers is also a reflection of the design approach that he has pursued over the years and the buildings that result.

Among Abe's generation there is no unifying aesthetic or philosophical approach. For some, material experimentation is a valid starting point. For others, structural innovation drives their designs. What Abe does share with his colleagues is an enthusiastic embrace of technological advance, an eagerness to engage with and not ignore the urban condition, a willingness to discard preconceived formal notions, and, in many cases, a love of football.

According to Abe, one of his most satisfying achievements was founding the A Cup, an all-architect football tournament that kicked off in Sendai in 2002 when Japan was stricken with World Cup fever. At the time a group of 25 architects who had assembled at Abe's university for a workshop decided to take a break from bantering about design, divide themselves into two teams, and kick a ball around. Today, the contest has grown to comprise 800 design aficionados who gather at a stadium outside Tokyo for one day each summer in the hope that their team will take home the championship.

For Abe the appeal of football is not just winning but how the game is played. Though shaped by a consistent

FA-1, Yokohama, Kanagawa Prefecture, 1995

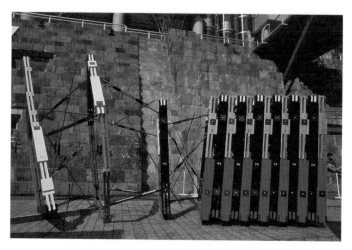

Shirasagi Bridge, Shiroishi, Miyagi Prefecture, 1994

Reihoku Community Hall, Reihoku,
Kumamoto Prefecture, 2002, exterior wall →

set of rules, the strategy and play of every match is different – just like architecture. Paralleling the game, Abe's creative process requires a playing field in the form of an arbitrary geometric model, a set of rules or design guidelines of his own choosing, a client with a specific site to put the ball in motion, and the goal of a completed project to bring it all together.

FA-1, a sculptural installation made in 1995, was a pure expression of many key components of that process. Abe started by creating a basic geometric unit: a 2 m (7 ft) square frame made of metal and wood held together by seven joints. With his students he then copied the frame 16 times and laced them together with sliding steel bars, resulting in a cube that fits inside a shipping container but could expand up to 15 times its length and 3 times its height. Essentially they designed the limits, or rules, of what shape it could be. For one week, FA-1 sat on display in a sunken courtyard at the base of a large commercial building in Yokohama, where its limbs were reconfigured daily, demonstrating the structure's remarkable ability to scale walls, fill corners and enclose a tunnel-like space.

FA-1 was designed as a work of art, but for Abe it was an important conceptual experiment that exemplified the freeze-frame-style, the repetitive unit method he devised to pinpoint and provide a focused response to local conditions. This approach appears repeatedly in Abe's portfolio of completed works, starting with the stadium and its contemporary, the Shirasagi Bridge. To support the stadium's irregularly curved grandstand that arches up above the ground plane, Abe encircled its base with a sequence of flying buttresses, each one slightly different but equally spaced. Resembling FA-1, the Shirasagi Bridge is enclosed on either side by a parade of fixed, but incrementally different, triangular frames that impart a strong visual identity to the existing bridge. On a much larger scale, Reihoku Community Hall is composed of a series of wooden ribs that define the building's anthropomorphic shell. Again, the profile of each rib varies but the interval between them is uniform. In all of these projects the individual units are tailored to the unique loading, material and site conditions. But in each one they add up to a very dynamic and unified whole.

The freeze-frame approach is the most explicit expression of Abe's notion that architecture is meaningful when its form is derived from the specific conditions of the site and the programme. But every element that comes from Abe's drawing board – be it a line, surface or volume – emanates from those conditions. And in every project, urban or rural, interior or exterior, Abe looks for those salient, shape-defining forces and finds a way to actively engage them in his design process.

For example, the Yomiuri Media Miyagi Guest House and the Miyagi Water Tower both extracted their forms

Yomiuri Media Miyagi Guest House, Zao, Miyagi Prefecture, 1997, rear facade

Miyagi Water Tower, Rifu, Miyagi Prefecture, 1994

← Toko, Orléans, France, 2006

from the ground plane – the dominant characteristic of their respective, non-urban sites. While the spiralling walls enclosing the house sit on top of and mirror the sloping terrain, the water tower was meant to appear as though it is covered by the earth's surface. Toko, a temporary installation Abe created with a group of students in France, comes at the idea from the other direction. Instead of taking cues from topography, the students used their own bodies to mould an artificial landscape out of styrofoam divided into hills and valleys shaped like arms and legs but unified by a coating of bright red paint.

Naturally, urban sites, which come with a whole different set of variables, including privacy from adjacent sites, require different responses. Especially since plots in Japan can be exceptionally tight and uncomfortable. But Abe is interested in interaction, not isolation. To define boundaries while preserving contact, Abe uses a variety of two-dimensional screening devices and three-dimensional compositional elements. Both intersperse solids and voids.

Though made of perforated metal, Abe's two pachinko parlour facades are merely fronts for concrete walls. But they were also important precedents for the restaurant interior of Aoba-tei. Turning an applied wall treatment into a space-defining device, Abe inserted a punched metal membrane into his client's two-storey space. Characterized by a pattern of perforations inspired by the leafy branches of the tree outside, the screen is still decorative. But, more importantly, it encapsulates the exclusive eatery's irregularly shaped volume generated by an existing emergency exit and other fixed conditions. In the process it assertively separates the restaurant from the base building's mundane concrete shell without severing their tie completely.

Similarly, an array of movable chessboard screens is the defining element of the restaurant interior of Dining Dayu, located in a nondescript bar building. This time the semi-permeable partitions – an even distribution of opacity and openings – double as movable walls that can divide the space into small rooms. This ability to balance exposure and closure explains why Abe chose alternating solid and glass panels for the outer walls of his 9 Tsubo House TALL as well. 'I wanted to diminish the dominance of the facade and build a strong connection between inside and out,' he says. At the same time static pattern-making is not his goal either. At Sasaki Office Factory for Prosthetics, the artificial limb factory occupying a flag-shaped site hemmed in by buildings, the exterior walls are recognizably chessboard-patterned. But their solid components, the reinforced concrete panels that support the building, vary in size according to loading and view. Abe comments, 'I wanted to control visual contact with the disordered surroundings.'

Abe has found that chessboards can achieve the same

Sasaki Office Factory for Prosthetics, Sendai, Miyagi Prefecture, 2004, street facade

9 Tsubo House TALL, Chigasaki, Kanagawa Prefecture, 2005, rear facade

Dining Dayu, Sendai, Miyagi Prefecture, →
2003, interior

result in plan. In the subsidized housing complex APH, mixed squares of building and garden (coupled with careful window placement) responded to the need for privacy as well as greenery for every tenant. APH followed in the footsteps of an earlier development composed of single-family homes and gardens laid out in a chessboard-like pattern but never realized. The only vestige of that master plan is M-House, a cross-shaped home whose four separate yards maximize contact between interior and exterior but minimize unwanted exposure, since the windows are set back from the street.

The use of perimeter courts and windowed, recessed niches to buffer interior space but let in light, air and a controlled view is one of Abe's preferred modes of bordering his buildings – be it a maternity clinic, dental office or one of many private homes. Instead of drawing a single, strong line, Abe's building edges are often intentionally weak and ambiguous, leading to a greater integration of indoors and out – a central tenet of traditional Japanese buildings that incorporate covered porches and courtyard gardens. 'We are not designing submarines,' jokes Abe. And so a boundary should not fully separate inside and outside but rather act as a mediator or interface between adjacent realms.

For Abe this means that boundaries are also the basis of form. 'To me a shape is a relative thing,' explains Abe. 'It is always the result of two conditions.' Or three or four in the case of the Kanno Museum. Contained within a cube of velvety brown Cor-Ten steel, the gallery interior barely interacts with its surroundings at all. Inside, however, the museum's eight rooms are piled on top of each other like soap bubbles, each one, in theory, completely dependent on its neighbours for definition – the ceiling in one room becomes a wall in another and so on. By conceptually pushing against each other the steel-enclosed volumes achieve a state of equilibrium preserved by the building's hard outer shell.

Kanno Museum marked a new direction for Abe. It not only required the invention of the cellular spatial structure, it also needed custom steel walls that were developed with the help of local shipbuilders. But Abe does not shy away from new ideas. In fact he actively seeks them out. A born risk-taker, Abe thrives on the stimulus of change even if, or maybe especially if, he does not know where it will lead him. But this doesn't mean he completely lets go of the old. One day he can be found inspecting grout on site in Sendai and the next on campus in California contemplating his multitudinous responsibilities as Department Chair. Straddling two cultures, two continents and two very different work environments isn't for everyone. But for Abe the move back to Los Angeles was a chance to enlarge his playing field, rewrite the rules, kick the ball around with a whole new team and, hopefully, score big.

M House, Haramachi, Fukushima Prefecture, 1999, facade

Sekii Ladies Clinic, Osaki, Miyagi Prefecture, 2001, west facade

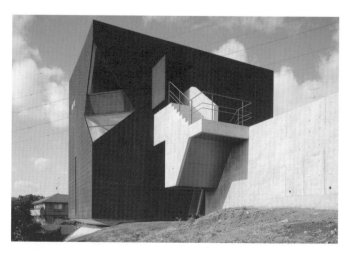

Kanno Museum, Shiogama, Miyagi Prefecture, 2005, stairs leading up to entrance

LINE

Line

For Abe, building design begins with geometry. Through the medium of lines, surfaces and volumes, he makes specific site and programmatic conditions visible and buildings that are inextricably joined to their place.

In response to these project specifications, Abe first devises a basic strategy and then selects a one-, two- or three-dimensional form to physically represent this conceptual design intent. From there he begins the creative process of transforming his idealized model into a distinct work of architecture.

Every scheme starts with a line, but conceptually many of Abe's buildings end there too. At the outset of his career, Abe literally extended the contour lines of the hilly landscape to generate the form of the Miyagi Stadium.

In addition to encircling space, Abe uses linear forms to connect or divide different realms. While the Matsushima Yacht House separates two areas, the Shirasagi Bridge links one side of the river to the other. Defined lengthwise by parallel walls or widthwise by a sequence of cross-section units, Abe's lines may be rendered in three dimensions.

N-House, a tube of space deformed by the site's extreme conditions, and Neige Lune Fleur, a restaurant interior whose inner walls tilt in response to existing building conditions, are both linear forms contained by parallel walls. But the Shirasagi Bridge and Reihoku Community Hall are accumulations of lateral ribs, each one slightly different and reflecting the local conditions. By the end of the design process Abe's initial linear response may have evolved formally, yet its vestiges remain embedded in the fabric of the finished construction.

Neige Lune Fleur, Sendai, Miyagi Prefecture, 1999.
Study models. →

Shirasagi Bridge, Shiroishi, Miyagi Prefecture, 1994

Miyagi Stadium [MSP]
Rifu, Miyagi Prefecture, Japan, 2000

When Abe was just 30 years old he made his dramatic debut by winning the international competition for the 49,000-seat Miyagi Stadium. Beating submissions from large construction companies and established design firms alike, Abe's triumphant proposal fused the stadium with its park-like setting located on the outskirts of Sendai. Two major events, the National Athletic Games of 2001 followed by the FIFA Japan/Korea World Cup of 2002, were the impetus for the competition. But Abe's game plan was to invent a new type of sports centre that would remain an integral part of the local citizens' functional as well as formal landscape long after the crowds stopped cheering.

'As a building type a stadium is ruled by the geometry of concentric circles derived from its basic requirement to act as a place where people can focus on its centre,' explains Abe. 'This resulted in a strongly fortified structure that separated spectators from the outside surroundings. My aim was to propose an open place without losing any functionality.' Since most large-scale stadiums are expensive to construct but occupied only a few times a year, Abe, who teamed up with Sendai architect Shoichi Haryu on this project, hoped to expand his building's usage by adding programmatic elements to draw people inside. But Abe could not attain all of his goals within the confines of the traditional stadium's static form.

The centrepiece of a large athletic complex that includes a pool, gymnasium and additional playing fields, Abe's stadium consists of two asymmetrical grandstands flanking the field in the middle. While the double-tiered main stand soars above, the single-tiered back stand rises out of the site's sloping ground plane. 'Gradually the hill turns into the stadium,' explains Abe. To underscore this point, Abe left the terrain behind the back stand all but untouched. A sequence of paved switchbacks slicing through the rough, natural grass connects the back stand's entrance to the ovoid circulation concourse that loops loosely around the building.

Accessible from multiple directions, the stadium may be entered in various ways and from all four sides. But most spectators climb a massive concrete ramp ascending from the concourse to the main entrance on the building's west side. This opening leads onto a broad corridor that rings the main stand's second floor as well as the top of the back stand and the exposed seating areas in-between. From this corridor, sports fans descend either up or down to take their seats. Additional ramps on either side of the back stand lead directly from the exterior concourse to the skywalk on the main stand's third floor, crossing paths with the internal corridor on the way up. Doubling as a public jogging course that threads through the building, this was intended to remain open even when the home team is away. 'You can walk your dog and peek inside at the same time,' jokes Abe.

The main stand may also be entered at ground level. In contrast to the cavernous, poorly utilized space below most stadium bleachers, the seven-storey underbelly of Abe's main stand is chock full of administrative offices, VIP rooms and assorted athletic facilities, many designated for public use.

Both the main and back stands are covered by two complementary but independent, crescent-shaped roofs. While the regularly shaped rear roof fits neatly over its seats, the main roof arches up gracefully towards the sky and extends beyond the bounds of the building below. At either end it terminates in a massive, steel-reinforced concrete block, one poised above the ground and the other grazing its surface.

The block's sheer bulk looks as if it could counteract the build-up of force generated by the swooping plane. But this effortless appearance belies the sophisticated system required to support the roof.

Unlike the relatively conventional cantilevered structure used for the rear stand, a 346 m (1,135 ft) long horizontal keel truss carries the main roof's steel-clad covering. Like a taut bowstring, a 2,000 tonne pre-stressed concrete beam buried underground ties the truss's two ends together, while 35 T-shaped vertical supports prop up its underside. Their tapered ends transfer the load to a series of triangulated concrete abutments that fan out from the building base like Gothic flying buttresses. In response to the varying stresses generated by the roof's complicated form and structural system, no two abutments could be shaped exactly same.

Even the geometry of the two roofs are not uniform all along their length – on both sides the smooth curved shape is actually a unique composite of many different arcs. These complex forms resulted from the explicit requirements for the number of seats and the angles needed for clear sight lines. Though the disposition of the seating differs on the two sides – the main stand holds 21,000 chairs and the rear stand 13,000 – these two factors determined their respective roof heights. In addition, the main roof had to be long and wide enough to cover one-third of the seats underneath. Instead of trying to force his roofs into pure forms – no single curve satisfied all of their dimensional requirements – Abe made geometry work for him by seamlessly blending different orders together. The building's incrementally different pieces were challenging to design and labour-intensive to fabricate, but their smooth connection yielded one very bold gesture.

Similarly Abe's choice and articulation of materials highlight the expression of the stadium's strong lines. Concrete's blunt surfaces and crisp edges work together with sleek steel panels to emphasize the overall shape of both stands. As Abe observes, 'Its like when you watch an ice skater, you can see that in each movement the parts of the human body work together.' Though distracting details are conspicuously absent, secondary building elements that cut across the building's powerful linear form were unavoidable. Abe tackled the main stand's vertical circulation with stairs made of steel that fit inside the large-scale building framework. Coated with a recessive gunmetal grey paint, the stairs are clearly a lower order of magnitude.

The realization of Abe's radical scheme required tenacity and verve. Yet throughout the design and construction process, Abe kept his eye on the ball. As a result of his clear vision and uncompromising execution, Abe was able to create a bold, record-breaking stadium.

Roof of main stand

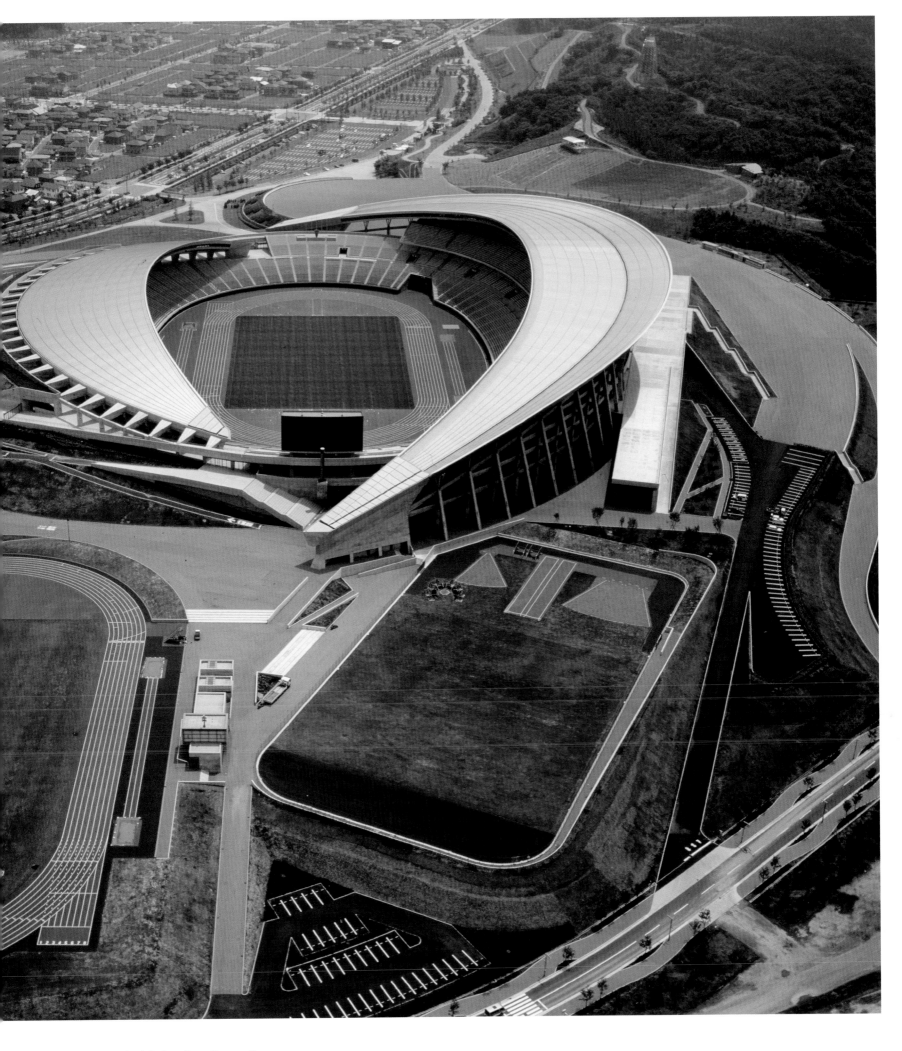

Aerial view from the north

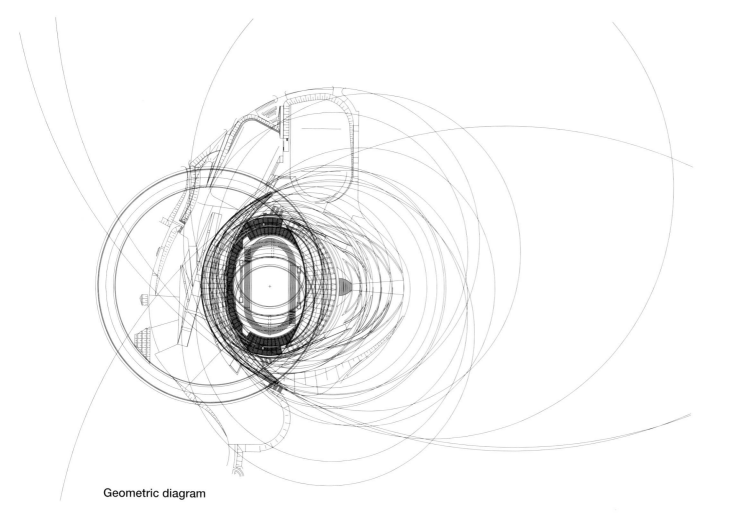

Geometric diagram

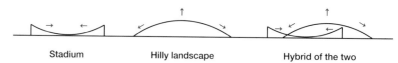

| Stadium | Hilly landscape | Hybrid of the two |

Conceptual diagrams

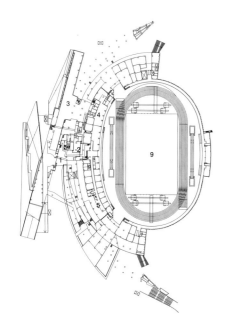

Ground-floor plan

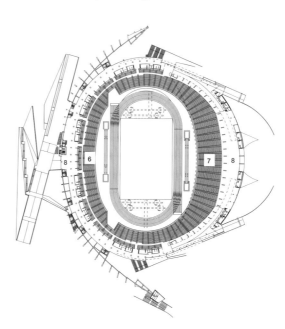

Concourse-floor plan

1   Main entrance
2   Office
3   Indoor track
4   Players' facilities
5   Conference room
6   Main stand
7   Back stand
8   Concourse
9   Playing field

Main stand (top), north end of main stand (bottom)

Main circulation concourse (top), main stand detail (bottom)

Playing field and main stand beyond (top), beneath the main stand (bottom)

Interior view of main entrance (top), indoor track (bottom)

Shirasagi Bridge [SBP]
Shiroishi, Miyagi Prefecture, Japan, 1994

Like many public commissions in Japan, the Shirasagi Bridge project started with a phone call out of the blue. This one came from a government representative from Shiroishi, a town of 20,000 in the middle of Miyagi Prefecture. Its purpose was to invite Abe to design the first in a series of civic works intended to revitalize the local economy and upgrade the community's public buildings. The project ear-marked for Abe, however, was not a school, library or bus stop. It was simply a handrail for a bridge. The bridge itself was beyond Abe's ambit. Though hardly a meaty commission, Abe, who had just returned from Los Angeles, made an enthusiastic proposal to the town's consortium of designers and bureaucrats overseeing the new developments. None of them had ever seen anything like it. When the mayor heard this rave review he gave Abe's design his immediate stamp of approval.

While the town may have initially envisioned a simple embellishment, Abe's handrail, which was completed in 1994, is a more powerful work of architecture than most full-fledged buildings. Composed of closely spaced triangulated steel fins that incrementally rise, fall and rotate all along the length of the bridge's two sides, it was intended, according to Abe, 'to create a spatial experience with a handrail'. Thanks to Abe's intervention, the bridge stands out against its background of modest homes and grassy fields where neighbourhood children fly kites and senior citizens walk their dogs. Though it connects the existing town with an area designated for new development, the two-lane bridge lined with pedestrian walkways on either side is more a local amenity than a major thoroughfare. Tying the man-made construction to the site's natural features, the ribs' undulating profile echoes the snow-capped mountains in the distance. At the same time, their reflective metallic surfaces relate to the shimmering water directly underneath.

The potency of Abe's scheme resulted in part from his relative freedom from the endless requirements inherent in building design. Yet it was hardly the product of unbridled creativity since the architect had to work within a number of very strict size, shape and weight parameters. The railing had to incorporate street lights illuminating the bridge from above, but it could not touch the river below. It could not interfere with either the standard-issue bumper-level guards designed to prevent errant cars from diving into the water. And it could not impinge on the bridge's overall structure lest a collapsed rail resulted in a failed bridge. Instead of viewing these conditions as limitations Abe treated them as shape-defining devices.

But translating these abstract ideas into a physical entity required the right medium. For Abe that took the form of 74 90-degree triangular trusses made of steel. 'I was interested in how I can generate a shape by tying them together,' explains Abe. He achieved this by establishing a set of design guidelines for himself. Principally, the length of the triangles' legs could vary proportionally but the right angle had to remain constant. This combination of fixed and variable qualities left leeway for practical adjustments yet ensured the geometric relationship among the triangles needed to unify and smooth out the entire composition. By gradually changing the triangles' dimensions and disposition along the 56 m (184 ft) length of the bridge, Abe created a sense of movement that matched the bridge's function of ferrying people and cars from one side of the Saikawa River to the other.

To keep the bridge user-friendly at night, the town planned for five street lights: two on one side and three on the other. Instead of simply adding pole-mounted fixtures Abe integrated the boxy lamps by attaching them directly to his triangular fins. In turn the lights' horizontal and vertical coordinates dictated the size and placement of the largest fins: the lights' 6 m (20 ft) height requirement established the fin tops and their 2 m (7 ft) distance from the edge of the bridge fixed the fins' maximum degree of rotation. Between these peak points Abe inserted sequentially smaller and then bigger rotating triangular ribs that cumulatively add up to the railings' dynamic wave formations. The transformation from smallest to largest happens gradually. But because of the uneven number of lights and the even number of ribs on the bridge's two sides, the profiles of the two railings are not the same: the wave frequency on one side is jagged while it is gentle on the other.

Since Abe also had to contend with a weight restriction, he knew from the start that he needed a range of triangles. If all 74 pieces had been the same height the railing would have been too heavy. Once the dimensions of the largest triangle were in place, Abe was able to calculate the smallest size needed to meet this requirement. To ensure a smooth transition between the two extremes, Abe constructed all of the pieces as similarly as possible. Each one faces outwards with a 400 mm (16 in) wide strip of shiny stainless steel that appears to be different colours but simply reflects light at different angles. Each strip is supported by metal-enclosed polyurethane backing to hold its shape and a galvanized steel truss to hold it up. Steel levers attach each truss to the wavy steel bar marking the top of the pedestrian handrail and to the concrete bridge below.

Yet assembling all of these pieces into a unified whole took some effort, as there were conflicting needs to satisfy. Where the triangles rotate inwards at the bottom Abe had to limit their contact with the bridge's concrete surface by removing bars from his railings. At the same time extra stabilizing elements had to be added as the triangles got bigger. Since Abe did not want these differences to show, he camouflaged them by discreetly extracting or inserting bars – even where they were not strictly needed for support. In the end Abe still had to shave off 200 grams from each truss to meet the rail's weight criteria.

Because every element used for the railings was contingent upon its neighbours, putting them together was a real balancing act. But in the end no piece looks out of place. The sum total is a sculptural place-maker whose dynamic form lures people across the water but makes them want to linger.

North facade detail

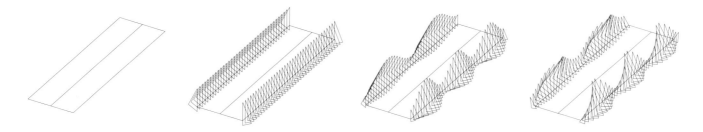

Conceptual diagrams

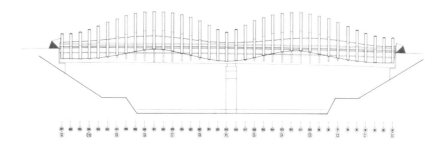

Elevation

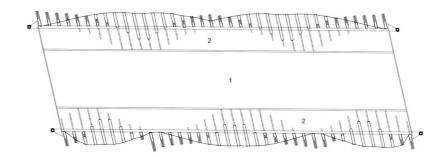

Plan

1 Road
2 Pavement

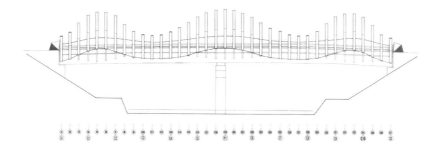

Elevation

View from south (top), street light detail (bottom)

South facade

Neige Lune Fleur [MRP]
Sendai, Miyagi Prefecture, Japan, 1999

In Japan, where dwellings are small and privacy well protected, people tend to socialize outside the home. Catering to this custom, unique multi-storey eat-and-drink buildings, each one loaded with tiny bars and specialized restaurants, have developed country-wide. Like many tenants of these commercial establishments, the proprietor of Restaurant Neige Lune Fleur dreamed of a strong street presence. But the interior space he acquired in a seven-storey building amid Sendai's burgeoning bar district was not only on the first floor. Its street face was completely obscured by the stair tower and the lift core located at the building front. Unable to project the restaurant outwards, Abe turned his attention inwards by creating a dynamic approach to the dining and drinking area – all within the confines of his client's 88 m^2 (947 sq ft) space.

This idea took the form of a corridor defined by two walls that twist and tilt all along their length, turning a simple conduit into a seamless series of subtly different spaces. Like the approach to a traditional shrine or temple, Abe's hall is much more than a straightforward organizational device or superficial decorative element. Delineating a clear separation between inner and outer realms, this path is a prelude to the meal. Dividing the rectangular room on its long axis, the corridor's slanted walls conceal the kitchen, lavatories and other secondary functions on either side while blocking the view from end to end. Only at the close of the journey are the five-table dining room and built-in bar revealed.

Conceptually the corridor started out as a simple tube of space, but prevailing programmatic conditions – the kitchen and bar needed more area, the lavatories less – deformed that straight line into a complex curve. Abe also had to navigate around ceiling-mounted plumbing pipes that service the tenant space above. In addition, the walls – conventional drywall clad with reddish maple veneer – had to comply with a host of specifications. For people to be able to traverse the hall the walls had to be parallel, no less than 1.2 m (4 ft) apart, and could not lean too much in any direction. The wall is truly vertical only at the entrance to the sequestered, four-person private room off to one side.

Physical requirements moulded the corridor configuration but, aside from the base building's outer walls, there were no predetermined criteria for deciding how to end the corridor's bold, sculptural form. Stopping it abruptly or extending it to the end of the room were both conceptually unacceptable to Abe. His solution was to treat the corridor's two surfaces as a single plane that bends acutely where it touches the far wall. He regarded this as a more sophisticated way to end. But because large wall sections were cut away to increase the dining and bar areas, the only manifestations of this idea are the inwardly inclined soffit above the bar and the shadow-concealed segment supporting it from below.

In contrast to the delicate tables and chairs perched primly on one side of the dining room, the five-seat counter is an integral part of the architecture. A steel sheet coated with clear finish, it is a horizontal extension of the wall's vertical wood plane. Crowning the counter overhead, an Abe-designed, x-shaped light fixture marks the restaurant's most desirable dining spot: in Japan, bantering with the bartender is an important ingredient of a good meal.

A bold statement rendered in a minimal, abstract way, Abe's interior design appears international and independent of its surroundings. But its setting, style of eating and even its name, which is a French translation of the poetic term *setsugekka*, expressing the appreciation of seasonal change, tie it closely to Japan.

Approach to dining area

Conceptual diagrams

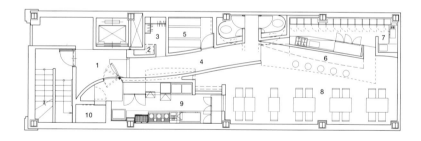

Floor plan

1   Entrance hall   6   Bar

2   Reception   7   Kitchenette

3   Cloakroom   8   Dining hall

4   Corridor   9   Kitchen

5   Private dining room   10   Storage

View towards built-in bar and dining area (top left), built-in bar (top right), dining area (bottom)

Matsushima Yacht House [MYH]
Matsushima, Miyagi Prefecture, Japan, 2000

An inspiration to poets, the subject of countless paintings and a major tourist attraction, Matsushima is one of the most celebrated natural landscapes in all of Japan. A collection of over 200 tiny windswept islands dotted with twisted pine trees, Matsushima has been regarded as one of the *Nihon Sankei*, or Japan's three most scenic spots, for centuries. Located off the coast of Miyagi Prefecture, the area was designated as a national park in the 1960s. Yet, as often occurs in Japan, unsightly food stands, souvenir shops and other commercial ventures have been allowed to encroach on the treasured landscape. So when the local government decided to build a combination park administration office/private yacht club on the property, Abe leapt at the chance to exert some damage control.

The government wanted an architect to develop and produce working drawings for an existing schematic design that placed the two entities side by side in a rectangular box. Convinced he could do better, Abe proposed reconfiguring the uninspired plan by splitting it down its long central axis and splaying the two functionally disparate halves in opposite directions. The idea was to distance the yacht club and the park office – an uneasy pairing at best – yet unite them end-to-end under one roof. Needless to say, the government eagerly accepted Abe's revised scheme.

Another problem with the government-issued scheme was that its boxy, object-like volume did not relate well to the site: a large, open parcel where the boaters' clubhouse, a pseudo-Western style cottage built after World War II, stood until it fell into disrepair. While there are no other buildings in the immediate vicinity, the land borders the club's boat slip as well as the much travelled access road leading to the historic sites and the docks where the island cruise boats are moored. Abe's objective was to use the building to hide the sight of the yachts from the tourists.

Located at the perpendicular intersection of two paths, one leading to the public harbour and the other to the private club, Abe's gently curving, single-storey building gracefully partitions the two realms. A simple but dynamic form, the long, wall-like structure is composed of two intersecting wings: one contains storage for 16 boats and the other the park's administration office as well as a conference room, lounge and lavatories used by both groups. Though the two parts do not connect inside, an external walkway running alongside the four shuttered storage berths turns into the building's internal corridor where the two wings meet. Paralleling this hallway, a covered, ramped walk hugging the facade's outer surface leads up to the building's main entrance.

While the two wings converge in plan, they diverge in section, both laterally and longitudinally, all along the building's 80 m (262 ft) length. The wings' galvanized steel roofs not only rise up steadily towards the buildings' outer extremities – each at its own pace, since the two sides differ in length – they also tilt side-to-side in opposite directions. Facing the harbour, the roof over the boat storage slopes up, opening the building to the water. But on the other side it slopes down in keeping with the scale of the window-wrapped corner conference room. At the front of the building, where it faces the public thoroughfare, one roof tilts down slightly, disguising the boats inside, and the other points skywards, inviting visitors to drop in.

Abe's strategy of splitting the government's proposed scheme in half not only yielded a narrow building. This approach also doubled its exterior surface, enabling direct access to the yachts from outside and increased natural light inside. Even the conference room, a communal space occupying the building's north-east corner, is washed with light from the south. Abe achieved this feat with two rows of clerestory windows, one internal and one external, aligned on an angle. Daylight enters the building through the high band of windows on the building's south face and passes through a second row of windows above the wall separating the conference room from the corridor. While the ceiling slants up, the solid partitions below are a constant height, leaving an open, wedge-shaped gap where rays can cross unimpeded from one side of the 10 m (33 ft) wide building to the other.

Because there are no neighbouring buildings and there is plenty of water close at hand, Abe built with wood. While a Glulam (glue laminated timber) frame held together with metal joints supports the building, cedar cladding stained a mellow dark brown encloses it. Understated and harmonious with the natural setting, the uniformly smooth, exterior surface accentuates the building's bold, sculptural form.

Initially, Abe may have been reluctant to merge public and private entities, but his building does a fine job of it. Within the yacht house each group has space of its own, but the two groups use other parts of the building in tandem. As Abe puts it, 'They have worked out a kind of time sharing system.' By banding together, both boaters and bureaucrats benefit.

Aerial view looking east

North elevation

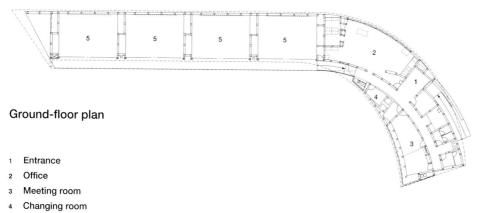

Ground-floor plan

1 Entrance
2 Office
3 Meeting room
4 Changing room
5 Yacht storage

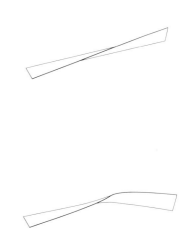

Conceptual diagrams

0	10

Site plan

0	20

View from the harbour

View towards boat storage (top), approach to
park administration office (bottom)

Park offices (top), entrance to park office (bottom left),
interior corridor (bottom right)

N-House [NH]
Kamakura, Kanagawa Prefecture, Japan, 2000

Topography is one of the defining factors for fashion and architectural designers alike. In the same way that neutral clothing assumes the shape of its wearer's torso, abstract architectural forms come to life when paired with hills, dales and other site-specific features. Though N-House's ultra-smooth, black concrete wrapping seems to conceal all irregularities of place and programme, the unusual curving volume was the direct result of coupling an idealized architectural form with an extensive client wish list and complicated site conditions.

The house is located in a Preservation District for Buried Cultural Assets in the middle of a well-known historic city within commuting distance of central Tokyo. This important designation explains why the tree-filled neighbourhood full of tasteful homes has remained unspoiled by excessive development. But it also meant Abe could not dig deeper than 60 cm (2 ft) unless his clients were willing to undertake an archaeological excavation at their own expense. Needless to say, they did not exercise this option. In addition to all the conventional lot-line setbacks, the steep cliff rising up at the rear of the site was a significant limitation requiring additional buffer space to reduce exposure to falling rocks. Building with reinforced concrete enabled Abe to inch closer to the mountain, but collectively these restrictions whittled his clients' generous 900 m² (9,688 sq ft) parcel down to an irregularly shaped 477 m² (5,134 sq ft) building site.

While grappling with complex external constraints, Abe also had to cope with the myriad internal requirements that his design-savvy clients put on the table. Because they had spent a considerable amount of time overseas, their list was an amalgam of Japanese- and Western-style elements that included tatami-floored rooms and discrete spaces for the kitchen, dining and living rooms – a stark contrast with most Japanese homes, whose public areas are not clearly divided. Yet the clients also wanted the feeling of spatial continuity. 'I like things one way but I also like things that are 180 degrees contrary,' in the words of the client.

Finding a way to balance these sometimes-conflicting requests and fit them inside the permitted building volume was not an easy task. Abe tackled this by creating a conceptual model and then modifying it to satisfy specific site and programmatic conditions. Abe's starting point was a simple chain of bead-like boxes – a more sophisticated version of the draped ribbon he used previously to design the Yomiuri Media Miyagi Guest House (see pp.84–91). The chain was composed of alternating solid and clear boxes symbolizing individuated rooms and interstitial spaces respectively.

The next step was to unite concept and reality by fitting the chain into the permissible horseshoe-shaped building footprint. The result came as a bit of a surprise. While the chains' ends splayed out freely in opposite directions, its compressed middle section buckled up – the consequence of forcing too much 'chain' into too small a space. The peculiar deformed shape was very dynamic but did not look anything like a house. Yet it appealed to the client and with a little massaging Abe was able to smooth out the overall form and translate the beads into bona fide rooms. What emerged was a sophisticated, exuberant building unfettered by structural grids and rigid geometric constructs. Governed by a logic and order all its own, the house consists of a string of rectangular rooms surrounding a dramatic double-height communal space.

The entrance is located where the two ends of the chain come together before splitting apart. Tucked between two curved, monolithic concrete blocks, the front door opens onto the foyer. From there, stairs lead first to the gallery and then to the living room, an airy, uplifting entertainment space. Off to one side is an intimate tatami-floored sitting room. To the other side is the Western-style dining area, an oversized alcove just big enough for a six-person table, which leads to the kitchen. Filling one end of the chain, the kitchen is equipped with under-counter refrigerated drawers, an angled sink accessible from two sides, and a host of other special features requested by the client. The other end holds one of two ground-floor guest rooms. Inspired by elegant European antecedents, a rounded stairway ascends to the first floor, where a balconied walk overlooking the foyer leads to the tatami-floored main bedroom and separate studies. While the wife's study is a contemplative retreat facing the back garden, the husband's hovers above the middle of the house, from where he can keep an eye on everything.

In contrast to the pure rectilinear rooms stacked up neatly around the perimeter, the communal area in the centre is a dramatic, free-form shape combining complex geometries. While the chains' distortions moulded its plan, Abe authored its undulating cover: a multi-curved, vaulted ceiling punctuated by two skylights that address practical acoustic requirements and ventilation needs in addition to the aesthetic expression of flowing space. The convex ceiling begins slowly above the gallery where its upwards slant parallels the stepped floor plane below. At the top of the stairs it gathers momentum, surging up to 4 m (13 ft) and then changing course to culminate in a wave-shaped surface that washes over the living room. The two very large operable skylights, one above the foyer and one in the living room, flood the house with natural light. Together daylight and double-height space unify the two floors and draw attention to the heart of the house.

Though Abe's conceptual solid–void pattern is less obvious inside, where slit windows and tiny transitional spaces set rooms apart from one another, it is quite visible on the front facade, which is composed of protruding rectangular boxes separated by deep recesses. In contrast to the arched rear facade, an artful composition of glass doors and windows looking out onto the ample back garden, the front facade is almost completely free of openings. Preserving the clarity of the architectural idea and the clients' privacy, windows are concentrated on the sides of the boxes – each one has three exterior exposures – where they are only obliquely visible from the street and look out in different directions.

The conspicuous absence of windows and the distinctive black concrete were not meant to be explicitly unfriendly but rather to keep the building from standing out. 'I wanted to make a building that blends in with its background,' explained Abe. Because of its plasticity, concrete was the logical material for realizing Abe's radical geometry, but the colour was strictly a matter of choice. Initially Abe envisioned covering the building with wood. But then he had a change of heart and decided to peel off the cladding – much to the contractors' surprise – and dye the concrete with pigment powder instead.

By contrast, the interior is light-hearted and relaxed. Though concrete makes another appearance inside the house – it is the primary flooring material downstairs – this time it is warm and welcoming. Smooth to the touch but mottled to the eye, the masonry surface is reminiscent of traditional, earth-toned Japanese ceramics. White walls accented by doors of different colours also contribute to the calm atmosphere.

To the untrained eye, N-House's bold, sculptural exterior may be an enigma. But its odd geometry is actually the logical result of a rigorous process to physically manifest invisible constraints.

Approach to front entrance

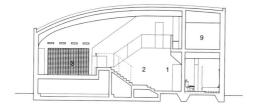

Section

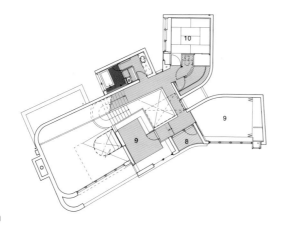

First-floor plan

Conceptual diagrams

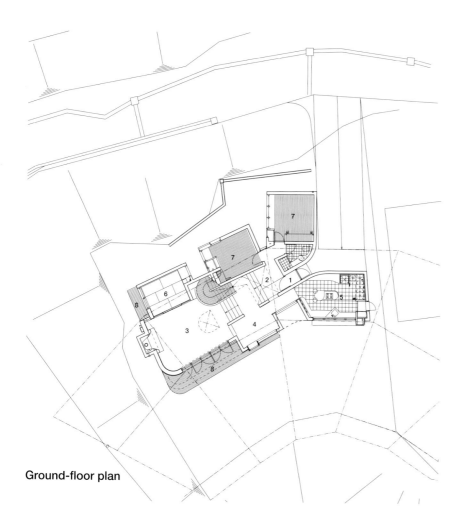

Ground-floor plan

1   Entrance
2   Gallery
3   Living room
4   Dining room
5   Kitchen
6   Japanese-style room
7   Guest room
8   Terrace
9   Study room
10 Main bedroom

0   5

View from garden

Three living room views

First-floor corridor (top left), foyer (top right), view from top of stairs (bottom)

I-House [IH]
Sendai, Miyagi Prefecture, Japan, 2001

Completed in 2001, I-House gives new meaning to the cliché 'a room with a view'. This is especially true in the context of urban Japan, where rooms with any kind of view are a relative rarity. Faced with densely built neighbourhoods and lax zoning laws, many architects strive to close off interior space and shield it from the surrounding landscape. But Abe took the opposite approach at I-House. Extroverted and encased in glass, the 264 m² (2,842 sq ft) home is enhanced by scenic vistas in almost every direction.

This unusual site and its sight lines were Abe's inspiration. Though located in central Sendai, the house is perched on a plateau in the middle of a broad valley studded with small-scale buildings. While neighbouring homes abut the house on two sides, the ground drops off precipitously elsewhere, opening the house to a sea of twinkling lights and a glimpse of the ocean in the distance.

Because of these spectacular views, the clients, an electronics company executive and his wife, purchased the 500 m² (5,382 sq ft) empty lot. Their highest priority was to build a hilltop home with plenty of open space overlooking the city. One of Abe's initial responses was to build them a glorified viewing platform. The tricky part was the 4 m (13 ft) vertical drop separating the site from the road. Yet Abe was not deterred. Instead of a conventional, horizontal slab, Abe conceived of his floor as a continuous surface that mirrors the ground plane even where it changes levels.

Due to the site's dramatic topography those changes were far from gradual. Though the bulk of the L-shaped house sits on a uniform plane, the main entrance had to be located at road level and, preferably, where the height differential between the two was the smallest. For the best views the living room had to be positioned as close to the cliff's edge as possible, and for maximum privacy the master bedroom had to be at the rear of the property. Once these key spots were positioned, the house's linear organization practically fell into place.

The medium that ties these points together is a conceptual tube of space that starts at the street-level front door. At the entry hall the tube becomes a grand stair that leads up to the main floor, pausing briefly on the way up at the wife's painting atelier off to one side. At the top of the stairs the tube turns into an expansive sweep of space containing the combined living room, dining room and kitchen. Capped by a soaring 3.2 m (10.5 ft) ceiling, the room is enclosed with rounded glass walls on three sides, like a fish bowl. The continuous glass sheet opens onto the stunning city view in two directions and the garden on the third. At the same time its curved surface gently reverses the circulation flow and directs it towards the rear of the room, assuming the shape of a tube once again. Here a few steps ascend to a narrow, glazed corridor leading to the house's private rooms: a tatami-floored guest room, the daughter's bedroom and, separated by a small courtyard, the master bedroom at the end of the hall. A lift down to the ground-floor entrance completes the circulation loop. Across from the bedrooms the glass wall opens onto the garden where a wood-clad ramp covers the grand stair below and leads to the roof terrace above.

Though spread out over four levels, I-House is actually only a two-storey building – together with the shared floor, a common ceiling unites the entire house, including the entry hall, stair and atelier. Only when closed doors conceal the private quarters is the continuity broken. Movement through the house follows a clear sequence, yet the glass-enclosed living room is open in every direction. Like a huge observation deck the airy, light-filled space visually expands out horizontally in a manner similar to many traditional houses, but is contained vertically by the ceiling and floor planes. This composition is underscored on the facade, where twin bands of painted aluminium panels front the roof eaves and wraparound terrace.

Reminiscent of the *engawa* porches frequently found in Japan's historic houses, the narrow terrace is covered with cedar planks that match the exterior wall panelling. The warm, reddish wood contrasts sharply with the strips of aluminium cladding above and below, as well as with the painted plasterboard walls and ceiling inside – the combination of wood and white surfaces is a common trait of many Abe-designed homes. In the main room the cedar decking segues into blonde wood flooring, but cabinetry and other vertical elements are covered in the same richly coloured wood used outside. Even the window frames are made of wood, but their vertical components not only hold the glass in place, they also conceal perimeter steel columns.

Because Abe was intent on maximizing the view, he wanted to minimize any intrusive structural elements as much as possible. He achieved this with an umbrella-shaped steel-frame system consisting of a series of horizontal steel spokes embedded in the roof that transfer their load to a solitary pillar standing in the middle of the living room. Where the spokes splay outwards at the building edge they connect with the slender steel columns hidden by the window frames. While a coat of white paint diminishes the pillar's presence, the perimeter columns' delicate dimensions – each one measures a mere 100 x 50 mm (4 x 2 in) – render them practically invisible. But this steel-frame structure by itself could not counter seismic and other sideways slippage.

'This system only works because the roof is connected to the floor,' explains Abe. Much more than a simple eye-catching device, the stair's swooping roof plays a critical role in the building's support system. Firmly anchored to the concrete floor slab below the bedrooms, the roof strengthens the whole house against lateral forces. By contrast, the front of the house appears to float. In fact, it does not even touch the ground at the property's outermost edge since Abe could not build too close to an existing retaining wall without disturbing the earth excessively. Instead he set the foundations back, well behind the wall, and cantilevered the house out as far as possible.

Despite the site's unique characteristics, I-House bears a certain likeness to the Yomiuri Media Miyagi Guest House and N-House, both designed shortly before. The resemblance to N-House is immediately apparent in the wavy roof used in both buildings. But conceptually all three are closely related. In each instance, Abe modelled an abstract way of living – a ribbon, a necklace and, at I-House, a tube of space – and allowed the site conditions to mould the idealized form. 'Because of the site's height changes I was more interested in the floor than the wall at I-House,' explains Abe. This marks a change in direction from the two preceding floor-based explorations but was a natural next step.

View towards living room

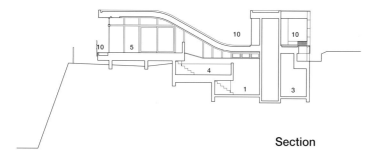

Section

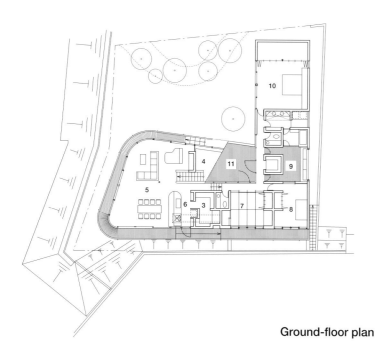

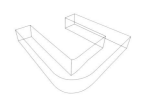

Ground-floor plan

Conceptual diagrams

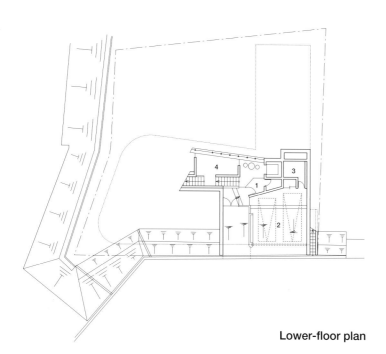

Lower-floor plan

1 Entrance
2 Garage
3 Storage
4 Atelier
5 Living/dining room
6 Kitchen
7 Japanese-style room
8 Bedroom
9 Terrace
10 Main bedroom
11 Roof deck

0   5

View from garden (top), view from street (bottom)

I-House   Two living room views

Atelier (top), roof slope (bottom)

Reihoku Community Hall [KAP]
Reihoku, Kumamoto Prefecture, Japan, 2003

For centuries the town of Reihoku's main claim to fame was the clash between Samurai warriors and Christian converts that took place on its soil. Despite its historical significance, this town of 9,000 located on a remote island off the coast of Kyushu, some 1,090 km (670 miles) south of Tokyo, is not exactly a tourist hotspot. But the 2003 completion of the town's community centre, designed by Hitoshi Abe in collaboration with Yasuaki Onoda, put it back on the proverbial map – at least the architect's version.

The community centre that Abe and Onoda built was part of the second wave of new architecture spawned by Kumamoto Prefecture's Artpolis programme. Established in 1988 by the prefectural governor, Morihiro Hosokawa, and his appointed commissioner, Tokyo architect Arata Isozaki, the programme aimed to raise the quality of public buildings throughout Kumamoto by inviting design-savvy architects from all over Japan as well as overseas to create everything from public lavatories to major museums. Though the programme succeeded in turning an agricultural backwater into an architectural mecca, some of the new construction met with mixed reviews from local citizens, while home-grown designers wondered why they were being passed over for these choice projects.

To counter criticism, subsequent commissioners, the Tokyo architects Toyo Ito and Teiichi Takahashi, made some adjustments to the Artpolis mission. Instead of simply imposing outsiders and their building programmes on the prefecture's towns and communities, architects were first assigned to talk with local citizens, find out what they wanted to build, and then, if all went well, design it for them. It was with this goal in mind that the commissioners dispatched Onoda, followed by Abe, to Reihoku.

An academic specialized in architectural programming, Onoda had worked with Ito on the planning of the Sendai Mediatheque, the Tokyo architect's masterpiece in downtown Sendai. Since the Kumamoto project needed the capability of a practising architect, Abe was brought on board. Together the two trekked down to Kyushu to meet the town mayor, who gave them a chilly reception at first. Their initial meetings with the local townspeople were not much better – it was not clear whether they would ever agree on what to build or whether to build at all. 'Everybody had a different opinion,' observed Abe. 'Some wanted a concert hall, some public housing and others an aquarium.'

But the one matter on which everyone saw eye-to-eye was the gaping hole that remained in the centre of Reihoku after its out-of-date city hall was rebuilt on a main access road at the edge of town. After three years of workshops and meetings to discuss what to do with the site, the townspeople concluded that they could not conclude. So they charged Abe and Onoda with the task of designing a community centre where they could continue their debate ad infinitum.

Because the planned project was a public amenity, Abe knew from the start that the building had to be economical, hence compact and multifunctional. Programmatically the project started out as two intersecting circles, one representing an auditorium and the other community meeting rooms. Where the two overlap Abe placed shared functions. Formally the architect conceived of the enclosure around these principal spaces as an idealized rectangular box. But as the programme developed and auxiliary uses, such as lavatories and dressing rooms, were added, it became increasingly clear that little boxes were needed as well. The question was how to join big and little together.

Abe's solution was to simply attach one to the other and drape the entire collection with wavy walls, integrating the whole group. Attached at the long edges of the flat roof, the walls splay outwards and ripple gracefully all along their length. A far cry from its simple boxy origins, the sophisticated building with its gill-like openings and sweeping window walls is at the same time alien and inviting.

Amazingly Abe achieved this dynamic result with locally sourced wood and glass. But the use of these materials came with restrictions, since they can only bend so much. As they worked they were constantly balancing function and materials. To achieve the undulating profiles, Abe built the curving surfaces with 90 cm (3 ft) wide faceted segments, each one angled slightly differently. Some are made entirely of wood. Others incorporate glass panes held in place by horizontal supports and vertical bars of timber. Because of its rigidity, the glass area had to reduce in size and the number of horizontal bars had to increase as the torque increased. 'Though it looks like we designed it this way,' says Abe, '[the shape reflects] the limitations of the material.'

Suspended from the building's main structure, the wavy walls pull on and put the roof beams into a state of tension, but they are not load-bearing elements themselves. That job is handled by a sequence of frames made from the laminated timber beams plus columns. Spaced an even 90 cm (3 ft) apart, the frames vary slightly all along the length of the building, recalling some of Abe's earlier works such as the Shirasagi Bridge and its steel triangles. The result is an irregularly shaped, column-free box measuring 14 m (46 ft) at its widest point. Within that box sits another wavy wall, this one made of 40 mm (2 in) square section wood bars and sound insulating material to ensure good acoustics in the auditorium.

While the theatre occupies one end of the oblong building, meeting rooms fill the other. In between the two are the information centre, an Internet café, an office, lavatories, and the Volunteer Bureau. A glass-enclosed box staffed by local residents, it serves as both the control centre for the theatre's lighting and audio-visual equipment as well as the management of the entire centre. In keeping with the building's open spirit, these functional pieces are loosely defined and flow easily from one to the other. Even the boundaries of the theatre are blurred by movable partitions that enable it to blend seamlessly with the other areas.

Though the theatre is the largest component, it does not dominate the building. Because the community centre caters for many different users, Abe tried to keep it as non-hierarchical as possible. It doesn't even have a main facade, let alone a main entrance. Instead multiple doorways are embedded in the folds of the exterior curtain wall, enabling access from different directions. Buffered by greenery and parking, the building is surrounded by a densely built mixture of post-war houses, commercial properties, and an elementary school whose pupils are delighted with their unusual-looking neighbour.

In Japan, multi-purpose public buildings like this one often fall prey to disuse, especially in small towns with limited resources and low populations. More often than not, the problem lies not in the building *per se* but with the expectations attached to it. But the citizens of Reihoku do not have their hearts set on performances by world-famous musicians and other blockbuster entertainments. Though they may not have realized it at the outset of the project, they are happy just to have a place for school band concerts, *omiai* parties for the introduction of prospective brides and grooms, and other everyday events.

Exterior wall, detail

South facade

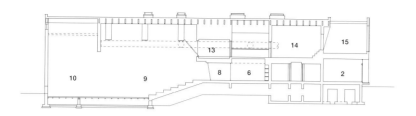

Section

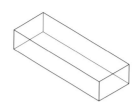

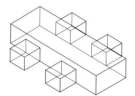

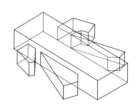

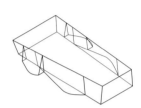

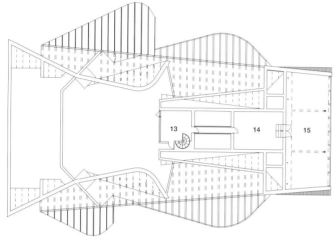

First-floor plan

Conceptual diagrams

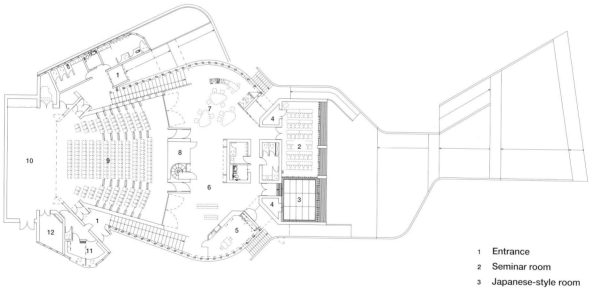

Ground-floor plan

1	Entrance	9	Auditorium
2	Seminar room	10	Stage
3	Japanese-style room	11	Dressing room
4	Storage	12	Storage
5	Office	13	Mixer room
6	Information corner	14	Mechanical room
7	Community lobby	15	Outdoor unit
8	Volunteer bureau		

0   10

Entrance (top left), exterior wall detail (top right),
south facade (bottom)

Reihoku Community Hall   Interior stair

Community lobby (top), view towards auditorium entrance (bottom left), view towards office (bottom right)

Reihoku Community Hall   Auditorium

SURFACE

Surface

To become a space-enclosing entity, lines must evolve into surfaces. But sometimes Abe skips this step entirely by starting with a space-enclosing plane as his design concept. To relate the Miyagi Water Tower to its hilly location, Abe envisioned it as a grass-covered bulge that emerges naturally from the ground. While the Water Tower stands amid open landscape, within constrained sites, either interior or exterior, Abe's continuous planes distinguish his space from its surroundings much like the manmaku traditional drapery used to temporarily delineate a special precinct. Instead of cloth, however, Abe's screening devices are made of wood, concrete or metal. And most incorporate patterned openings or perforations that filter views but provide visual texture and maintain a connection to the context. Though they are hard materials, Abe's screens behave like fabric by bending to fit or cover the base building's underpinnings, such as the facade of the pachinko parlour PTI, or the property's quirky outline in the case of the artificial-limb company headquarters, Sasaki Office Factory for Prosthetics. Spanning two floor levels with a jog in plan, a punctured metal screen unifies the space belonging to the restaurant interior of Aoba-tei. Lit from behind, it also imbues the exclusive eatery with a unique atmosphere that is remarkably removed from its mundane setting.

Sasaki Office Factory for Prosthetics, Sendai, Miyagi Prefecture, 2004. Study models. →

Aoba-tei, Sendai, Miyagi Prefecture, 2005. Interior stair.

Miyagi Water Tower [MWT]
Rifu, Miyagi Prefecture, Japan, 1994

Some royalty get palaces built in their honour. Others get water towers. To commemorate the wedding of Japan's Crown Prince and Princess in 1993, Miyagi Prefecture decided to erect a new storage tank to supply water for the stadium Abe was designing nearby. While the local government needed a conventional storage structure, they wanted a symbolic monument for the tree-studded recreation park surrounding its hilltop site.

'Since water towers always stand out, I wondered how I could build one that would respect nature at the same time,' pondered Abe. This one was certainly not going to be any exception, since it had to be 27 m (89 ft) tall, situated above the stadium, and capable of supporting a 91 tonne (100 ton) capacity tank. As with the stadium, Abe and his co-architect, Shoichi Haryu, coped with these tough conditions by blurring the boundary between architecture and landscape, and opening the buildings to the public, even though access to stadiums and water towers is usually limited. More continual-use sports facility than shuttered soccer arena, the stadium was meant for joggers and families as much as star athletes. And at the water tower they envisioned visitors entering at the front, ascending to the viewing platform and then down a second set of stairs to the exit at the back.

While these unconventional, user-friendly traits made Abe's water tower design more appealing, there was no getting around its awkward form. To lessen its presence and dissolve its unwanted monumentality, Abe decided to build with steel components that become progressively smaller towards the tower's perimeter, and to cover the structure with ivy to meld it with the earth.

The core of the tower's oval plan is the tank, a prefabricated metal drum, and its elaborate support system. Since the water delivery system relies on the pressure from a full tank to circulate properly, the hulking vessel had to be raised above ground where it would be elevated above the highest space it supplies – the facilities in the VIP suite that sits at the top of the stadium. Because this top-heavy configuration is especially vulnerable to earthquakes, it had to be offset by a massive, pancake-shaped foundation that could disperse its load over a large area. Between the tower's top and bottom, hefty columns direct vertical forces downwards. In turn, 15 trusses pull outwards and secure the columns, 'like a tent at a camp site', according to Abe. The two systems are bound together by two rings that support platforms for the tank and the viewing deck respectively. The entire construction is wrapped with a cone-shaped lattice made of flat steel bars. Covered with ivy, the woven surface would appear as a delicate membrane gently plucked from the ground.

Unfortunately this idea was literally nipped in the bud when an overzealous maintenance crew inadvertently tidied up the nascent vines. 'If the ivy had been allowed to grow,' explains Abe, 'conceptually it would have been like looking out from beneath the surface of the earth.'

Without its coat of greenery, Abe's bare bones structure bears some resemblance to the electrical towers in the distance. Yet the lacy, steel cone still achieves Abe's goal of building a monument by making a tower disappear.

Steel lattice enclosure

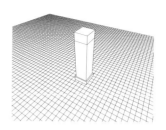

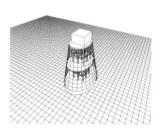

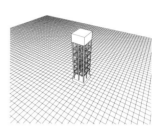

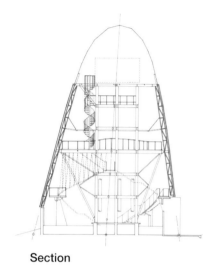

Section

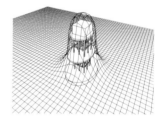

Conceptual diagrams

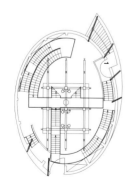

Lower-floor plan

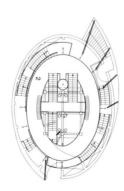

Upper-floor plan

Roof plan

1   Entrance
2   Observatory

Tower seen from afar (top), concrete base (bottom)

Miyagi Water Tower — Internal stairs

Structural steel core

Yomiuri Media Miyagi Guest House [YG]
Zao, Miyagi Prefecture, Japan, 1997

A swirl of sharp corners and slanting planes, the Yomiuri Media Miyagi Guest House is both oddly familiar and comfortably alien. Though the dynamic, dark-wood building looks as if it could have dropped out of the sky, it actually grows out from the earth. Echoing the contours of the site's sloping topography, a 90 m (295 ft) long board and batten wall defines the house, first wrapping its perimeter and then looping around a second time to encircle the double-height living room at its heart.

Commissioned by an advertising executive from Sendai, the house is located in a *bessochi*, or second-home development, at the base of Miyagi Prefecture's Zao Mountain. The typical Japanese *bessochi* is a large land parcel purchased and divided by a developer, who adds access roads, brings in utilities and takes care of many of the initial complications of building in the countryside. This somewhat sanitized version of nature is then marketed to future homeowners who purchase a site from the developer and usually hire the recommended contractor to build the house. But this client wanted something more. To make the most of his 1,392 m² (14,983 sq ft) plot he knew he needed a skilled architect who could think outside the box.

In contrast to the typical urban site in Japan, where tough surrounding conditions, stringent code issues and small plot size severely reduce design possibilities, this property came with very few restrictions. Aside from a few unobtrusive houses nearby, the only controlling factor was a limit on the number of trees that could be cut down. Unfettered by rules and regulations, Abe got his design foothold from the land itself.

Because the property slopes down towards a ravine to the south, the building's basic orientation was immediately clear. What was not so obvious was where exactly to put the house – this required a close study of the hill's profile. 'We started with a conventional process,' explains Abe, 'but nothing seemed quite right.' Wherever the rectilinear study model came in contact with the contoured site model there was friction. In short, the two did not meld at all. It became clear that he needed to loosen up the boxes and break up the form of the building to make it fit with the landscape.

This quest led to the removal of the boxy, cardboard mock-up's top and bottom, followed by the unfolding of its four walls. This simple act freed Abe from fixed corners and static surfaces. And it turned a standard-issue study model into a brand new design tool: a flexible ribbon of cardboard. Ripe with possibilities, the ribbon could be lengthened, widened and bent at any angle, as well as cut, to conform to the topography. By starting with a simpler, more abstract design medium – a two-dimensional surface as opposed to a three-dimensional volume – Abe was able to effectively unite terrain and built form.

Another important consideration that also helped pin the building in place was its approach from the road. 'How to reach the front door is very important to me,' explains the architect. Here again Abe looked to the land. Instead of relying on a fence or gate to mark the entry, Abe aligned the house's north face at an angle to the natural ridgeline running along the site's north side. Where these two lines converged Abe placed the entrance. Made of dark wood, the door itself blends with the exterior wrapping. But both the wood decking on the ground and the downward-sloping facade articulate a strong sense of perspective that points the way inside.

Contained by the wood band, the house's interior consists of a double-height living room surrounded by subsidiary spaces for eating, sleeping and making the transition from the outside. A place to re-orient sight lines and circulation, the foyer facilitates a smooth passage from the wooded exterior to the wood-lined living room. A hybrid space with a cosy fireplace nook in one corner and a louvred ceiling overhead, the triangular room is both the family gathering place and a neutral backdrop for seminars, presentations and other business-related events. Sheltered and womb-like, the room is practically windowless – a single fixed sheet of glass offers the only direct view outside. But where the double-height room abuts the single-height dining space Abe replaced the wall and timber frame structure with a sturdy steel beam, enabling an unimpeded flow between the two functional zones. Flanked by an alcove-like kitchen and a bathroom suite, the dining area opens onto an expansive, wedge-shaped, covered porch overlooking the ravine. The sleeping quarters, a tatami-mat room that can accommodate 20 futons, and a Western-style bedroom belonging to the owner, are upstairs.

While the house reads as an integrated whole, the wall, whose dark-brown surface is clearly visible both inside and out, is its essential, defining feature. Inspired by the conceptual cardboard strip, the wall's changing height mirrors the subtle rises and falls of the ground below, sometimes decreasing as it wraps the house perimeter and then spiralling up to surround the living room and first-floor sleeping areas. Within the house these fluctuations create a programmatic hierarchy and distinguish spaces of different character – the living room's high walls and angled ceiling attest to its importance.

Complementing the height variations, the wall's construction also underscores the sense of movement and differentiates usage. The outer wall consists of slender, evenly spaced vertical supports and angled horizontal planks whose slanting lines guide the gaze up or down, or hold it flat where the wall turns into the screen-like porch enclosure and the boards are reduced to thin strips. Inside the house, the wood surface is largely decorative. While its uniform colour ties the rooms together, Abe used a range of different materials, such as white stucco and black painted steel, to delineate elements like the stair enclosure and the fireplace flue respectively.

Despite its irregular geometry, this predominantly dark-wood house invites comparison with traditional architecture. In addition to its timber construction the house is fitted out with iconographic elements like an *engawa*-inspired porch and *shoji* screens. While the connection to history may have pleased the client, who grew up in a *minka* farmhouse and requested the tatami floor, the link was more incidental than intentional for Abe. 'I cannot deny that I am influenced by Japanese traditional buildings,' comments Abe. 'But I did not want to recreate one. I wanted to use available construction methods and materials.'

The most compelling explanation for Abe's dark walls, however, circles back to his initial vision of relating architecture and landscape. When he first stood at the edge of the site and looked towards the ravine he saw many different shades of green. But further back he could see only dark brown. While the wall does a good job of partitioning inside and out, its dark wood ties it back to the natural environment.

Rear facade

Section

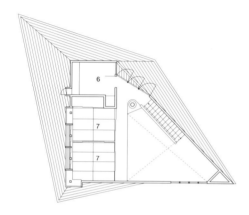

First-floor plan

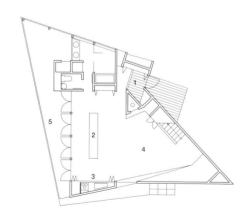

Ground-floor plan

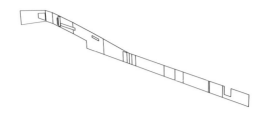

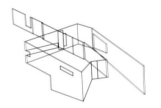

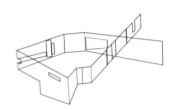

Conceptual diagrams

1 Entrance
2 Dining room
3 Kitchen
4 Living room
5 Deck
6 Western-style bedroom
7 Japanese-style room

West facade (top), main entrance (bottom)

View from the ravine

Yomiuri Media Miyagi Guest House Screened porch (top), living room (bottom)

Stairs connecting living room to first floor

Michinoku Folklore Museum [KIR]
Kurihara, Miyagi Prefecture, Japan, 2000

In its mid-twentieth-century heyday, Kurihara, a town of 20,000 in rural Miyagi Prefecture, was a major rice collection point that shipped the locally grown crop to Sendai, Tokyo, and points beyond. During the post-World War II period the upgrading of roads and re-routing of train lines led to improved distribution networks country-wide. But after these changes Kurihara was no longer an important hub and the town's economy steadily declined. An added blow was the precipitous drop in tourism that accompanied the construction of a bypass road connecting the bullet-train station on one side of the town with mountains on the other, completely circumventing its centre.

As the boarding up of Mom-and-Pop stores along Kurihara's main streets increased and the local train service decreased, the town government realized they needed to launch a concerted revitalization effort. Recycling the abandoned rice warehouse opposite the depot as a museum of regional history was a good place to start. Constructed of local volcanic stone in 1933, the centrally located 392 m² (4,219 sq ft) storage vault not only recalled the town's earlier prosperity, it had the potential to become a symbol of Kurihara's rebirth. But uncertainty surrounding its structural viability – no one knew whether it conformed to the contemporary standards required of a public facility – led the town officials to structural specialist Junichi Onose of the Tohoku Institute of Technology and his colleague Hitoshi Abe. Together they studied the building's condition and then Abe stayed on to design its renovation and extension.

Though its structure had never been formally calculated, the masonry building reinforced with an internal, surface-mounted timber frame had stood the test of time and even survived the Miyagi Bay earthquake in 1978. But it was not entirely problem-free. While the rectangular building's 14 m (46 ft) sides were short enough to withstand seismic forces, its 28 m (92 ft) sides needed supplemental bracing to prevent future failure in the middle.

Abe's response was to sandwich the two long walls and their adjacent wood columns with steel beams, one exterior and one interior. He then inserted steel trusses at the existing walls' one-third points that span the width of the warehouse and connect the new internal beams. 'It is like a sumo wrestler sitting in the middle of a building with one hand pushing against each wall,' explains Abe. Bracing each truss at one end is a steel buttress that transfers its load to concrete foundations buried beneath the extension.

'The structure was a big issue,' explains Abe, 'but I did not want to express it explicitly.' So he encased the trusses and buttresses with wood panels stained dark brown to contrast with the stone's golden colour and rendered the new structural scaffolding as a two-storey, space-defining architectural element. Embedded among the existing cedar columns, Abe's intervention bolsters the old structure. But it also turns the warehouse's raw space into the 898 m² (9,666 sq ft) museum's four galleries, three at grade and one at mezzanine level, and outlines the circulation loop that ties the existing building to its addition at the front of the site.

In contrast to the warehouse's solidity, the C-shaped new construction made of glass, steel and blonde wood panelling is light and airy. Containing the museum office, café and shop, it is angled towards the station plaza across the street and also embraces a courtyard linking the museum's two parts together. Sight lines from the open entry area and parking lot in front of the building extend straight through the new extension, into the courtyard, and across to the warehouse. Intended both as a place to appreciate the historic building and as a venue for outdoor events, the asphalt-covered precinct is not only open to the sky but also to the public promenade running along the north side of the site, where sliding, slatted wood screens barely separate the architectural and urban spaces.

While the warehouse is a static rectangular box, the dynamic extension is irregularly shaped both in plan and section. Reminiscent of the Yomiuri Media Miyagi Guest House, it spirals around three sides of the courtyard but is visually anchored in the old building – at the rear, the new roof tilts up to fit neatly beneath the warehouse's first-floor cornice line but slopes down in front where it hovers above the single-storey office inside. Where building interior meets exterior courtyard, the outer skin consists of sliding glass doors that may be pushed aside. Standing outside the movable walls but flush with the overhanging roof eaves, fin-shaped columns point towards the warehouse and echo the extension's angled walls. Within the new building, fixed elements are few and far between except for wall-mounted, glass-fronted cabinets intended to showcase museum shop merchandise.

Similarly, within the warehouse Abe limited permanent alterations and walls to the wood-covered steel scaffolding. Stained dark to match, wooden partitions may be inserted beneath the mezzanine to reconfigure the space and wheeled display cabinets are designed to vary the installations.

'We thought the building itself was a beautiful artefact,' says Abe. But it needed cleaning, restoration and retro-fitting to render it habitable. To illuminate the nearly windowless interior Abe punched out the new galvanized steel roof and added clerestory openings as well as electric fixtures mounted to the tops of the existing wood beams, which bathe the entire room with soft light. And floor heating as well as smoke detectors were needed for comfort and safety. At the same time, Abe salvaged and spruced up the warehouse's original fittings, such as its hefty metal doors, wherever possible.

Though big boned and object-like, this new structure does not interfere excessively with the fabric of the existing building. Instead, it works together with the old warehouse to breathe new life into a relic from the past.

View from ground-floor exhibition room

Section

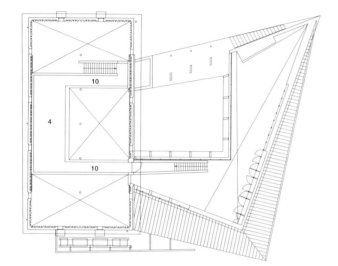

First-floor plan

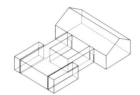

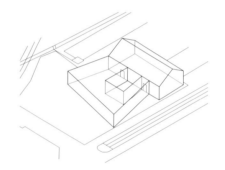

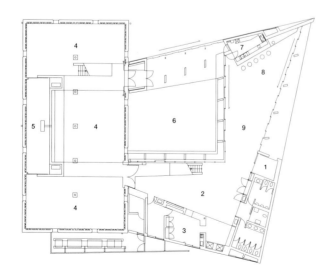

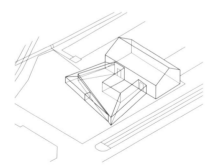

Conceptual diagrams

Ground-floor plan

1	Entrance	6	Courtyard
2	Gallery/shop	7	Kitchen
3	Office	8	Café
4	Exhibition room	9	Lounge
5	Storage	10	Bridge

0   5

East facade (top), north facade abutting warehouse (bottom)

Michinoku Folklore Museum Gallery and café

First-floor exhibition room (top left), ground-floor exhibition room (top right), courtyard (bottom)

Existing wood frame and new structure in exhibition rooms

Sasaki Office Factory for Prosthetics [SOB]
Sendai, Miyagi Prefecture, Japan, 2004

In recent years the manufacture and technology of prosthetic arms and legs has progressed rapidly. Despite these technical improvements, artificial limbs still conjure up images of archaic, ill-fitting orthopaedic devices. Determined to erase this stigma, the owners of Sasaki-Gishi Prosthetic and Orthotic Services envisioned a day when the perception of their products – well-designed devices to aid mobility, not substitute body parts – would catch up.

The realization of this dream started when the city of Sendai decided to enlarge the road in front of their existing factory and asked the company to relocate. In exchange for their dingy, out-dated timber building near one of the city's major hospitals they got a bright, state-of-the-art combined office and factory on the edge of downtown Sendai. Completed in 2004, Abe's 866 m² (9,322 sq ft) facility fills a flag-pole-shaped site squeezed between a dental clinic painted eye-popping emerald green and a car dealership whose plate-glass windows showcase Toyota's latest offerings. Wrapped with understated chessboard walls made of concrete and glass, Abe's building makes no attempt to compete with its garish neighbours. But it does not retreat either. A mere 7 m (23 ft) wide, the facade is the narrowest of the building's six facades. Yet its bold, symmetrical composition compensates for its size. Punctuated by clear panes, the building face offers passers-by glimpses of the factory's inner workings without explicitly advertising its products or attracting unwanted curiosity seekers.

Another complication impacting the facade was the need for user-friendly parking on site. Since the modest front facade is the only place the site abuts a street, Abe had no choice but to put the garage access in this prominent place. He did so by simply omitting the base of the front wall – a clever move that gets the job done without emphasizing vehicle traffic in and out of the building. Instead the driveway is hidden in shadow and the block of upper floors appears to float.

Running the facade's full width, the driveway leads directly into the building's ground level, a single, semi-exterior space that contains parking for two or more cars as well as a practice area composed of patches of gravel, stone and brick where clients can try out their new appliances. Creating what Abe terms a 'soft boundary' between inside and out, the porous perimeter walls partially shield the ground floor but a 6 m² (20 sq ft) courtyard at the heart of the building opens it completely to the sky.

'Basically [this project] is two parallel buildings with an open space in the middle,' explains Abe. One is designated for company administration and the other for product manufacture. Yet because the glass-walled, three-storey void is all that separates the two halves, even the divided upper levels seem connected. While glazed corridors and galley kitchens doubling as circulation conduits physically join the two halves horizontally, a concrete lift core wrapped with glass-enclosed stairs connects the floors vertically.

The building is entered at grade but the reception area is one floor up, adjacent to the administrative office and consultation rooms and opposite the factory's plaster and lamination rooms, dressing rooms, lavatories and storage areas. On the second floor the company president's office and a 24-seat seminar room fill the administrative half, while the fabrication and finishing rooms, where final adjustments are made to the life-like limbs, can be seen across the void.

Thanks to the transparent core, unimpeded sight lines stretch from one side of the building to the other, binding the two halves together visually. The glass-encased void and partial-glass partitions separate different programmatic pieces but unify the interior and allow daylight to permeate throughout. As they are measured and fit, clients can look across at technicians moulding, sanding and adjusting arms and legs made of plaster and plastic. Exposing this painstaking process demystifies the off-putting associations with prosthetics and underscores the craft involved in their manufacture – each custom-made limb is built largely by hand. Instead of cold and clinical, this open, relaxed environment is warm and welcoming.

Hollowing out the middle of the building not only yielded good results inside. It also helped Abe cope with his tight, awkward site. 'If a building opens onto the wall next door, it feels depressing,' observes Abe. Positioned above or below but never at eye level, the glass panes on the outer wall look out at abstract snippets of the neighbouring buildings only inches away. But the building's primary focus is inwards and away from the surrounding conditions. Another benefit of the void space is that it enabled Abe to build out to the property lines (less some tolerance for the ease of construction), while complying with the maximum floor-area restrictions required by code.

Outlined with walls made of alternating post-tensioned, pre-cast concrete and glass panels, Abe's L-shaped building appears extruded from the site. Structure and enclosure all-in-one, the walls eliminated the need for internal columns or lateral bracing. With the help of slabs and beams they carry the building's vertical and seismic loads. Unlike conventional masonry systems consisting of stacked elements, the factory-made panels do not derive the bulk of their strength from compression. Laced with steel tie rods tightened on site, the panels, which range from 18 to 30 cm (7 to 12 in) in thickness, work primarily in tension.

At first the chessboard walls read as a uniform cladding. But Abe has a penchant for creating rules and then accommodating them to the particularities of place and programme. Offsetting the walls' static grid pattern, subtle variations in panel size and position enrich the building's surface and quietly express underlying conditions such as internal room dimensions and partition placement. The most visible irregularities by far, however, are those caused by the eccentric loading conditions generated by the void in the middle of the building.

In lieu of standard framing elements at the roof level, two 14 m (46 ft) long, truss-like beams bracket the opening. Because of the concentration of force where the beams transfer their loads to the perimeter walls, Abe had to strengthen the vertical support. He achieved this by intersecting instead of staggering the wall panels below these four points. Collectively the overlapping concrete plates behave like columns that direct the pent-up force down to the foundations.

In contrast to the masked exterior, the building's working parts are largely exposed inside. Concealed by white paint only, layers of corrugated steel deck, rounded pipes, boxy ducts and spindly lighting tracks complete the interior. Reminiscent of nineteenth-century industrial buildings, the building's exposed innards enabled Abe to meet the 10 m (33 ft) height restriction stipulated by the code. If there had been a ceiling it would have needed to be quite low, so Abe thought it better not to have one at all.

This honest expression of the building's machine-like parts may be grounded in practicality. But bodies, like buildings, are assemblages of functional components that sometimes need additions or reconfiguration to improve performance. And this should be nothing to hide.

Glass-enclosed central space

Second-floor plan

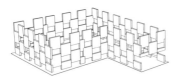

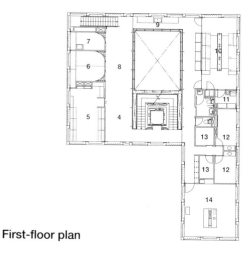

First-floor plan

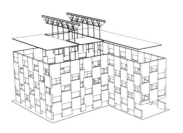

Conceptual diagrams

Ground-floor plan

1	Parking	12	Changing room
2	Entrance	13	Storage
3	Testing area (exterior)	14	Lamination workshop
4	Waiting area	15	Welding workshop
5	Office	16	Mechanical workshop
6	Fitting room	17	Technician's workshop
7	Casting room	18	President's office
8	Testing area (interior)	19	Library
9	Kitchenette	20	Meeting room
10	Plaster workshop	21	Storage
11	Laundry	22	Seminar room

Street facade

Sasaki Office Factory for Prosthetics

West facade

Plaster workshop (top), first-floor corridor (bottom)

Truss and steel bar from which the floors are hung

Aoba-tei [AIP]
Sendai, Miyagi Prefecture, Japan, 2005

In Japan, Big Macs and café lattes are ubiquitous, but towns country-wide still proudly produce food specialities all their own. Thanks to the enduring popularity of the Sendai delicacy, beef tongue, the Abe-designed restaurant Aoba-tei came into being. Having amassed a fortune by introducing a pre-packaged version of the cow bi-product to Japan's lucrative gift food market, a local tongue tycoon hired Abe to create the interior for an upscale eatery that would distinguish their shared home town in a sophisticated way. Encapsulated by a perforated steel screen backlit by hundreds of tiny bulbs, the dramatic S-shaped space contrasts sharply with the smoky bars and dark drinking establishments where tongue traditionally tops the menu.

Completed in 2005, the 220 m² (2,370 sq ft) Aoba-tei occupies the bottom two floors of an innocuous, seven-storey commercial building. Abe's client leased the space after the previous tenant, a fast-food outlet, closed down. Located across from Toyo Ito's Sendai Mediatheque, the base building faces Jozenji Street, one of Sendai's lovely, tree-lined boulevards.

Restaurant patrons enter directly from the street into Aoba-tei's ground-floor reception area, where the slanted ceiling subtly draws people inside. From there a free-standing stair leads up to the 30-seat dining room, dominated by a massive, wooden counter. Echoing the steel screen's double-barrelled section, the counter's snaking form incorporates a bar at one end, an open grill at the other, and seating in-between where diners can graze on Aoba-tei's French-inspired cuisine while chatting with the proprietor – an important ingredient of a good meal in Japan. Behind the counter, but barely visible through Abe's screen, is the kitchen designed by Aoba-tei's own celebrity chef. Towards the front of the restaurant the ceiling tilts up to orient the room to the street. Here free-standing tables provide additional seating and enjoy unimpeded views of the foliage outside.

Forging a direct relationship between his interior space – 'Aoba-tei' means 'leafy, green place' – and its urban context was paramount to Abe. But drawing a clear line between the new restaurant and the existing building was equally important. While he could not tamper with the building's glass and steel curtain-wall facade, its grade-level main entrance or the fire escape balcony upstairs, he was able to cut a hole in the floor and join his two-storey space internally. He wanted the connection between the two floors to be very smooth to make it feel like one space, and he thought an inner skin would make that connection.

Playing off the base building's benign straight lines and neutral material palette, Abe's rust-coloured steel membrane envelopes Aoba-tei, physically separating the restaurant from its immediate surroundings but uniting its two floors into a single, complex volume. Because of the locations of the base building's entrance and fire balcony, Abe could not stack his two floors congruently. Instead he built two pods that overlap in section, and delineated their shifted profile with the continuously curving steel surface.

Moving seamlessly from walls to ceiling, the screen wraps both sides of the reception area, squeezes through the floor opening and balloons out on either side of the dining room upstairs. Where the screen bends and conceptually covers the first floor, Abe replaced it with walnut planks. Exceptionally thin and full of holes, the steel sheet could not stand up to steady foot traffic.

Inspired by the zelkova trees outside, the screen is like a Seurat painting. From up close its holes appear as random dots, but from further away the dots coalesce and an abstract representation of leaf-covered limbs and bifurcating boughs comes into focus. Though the overall end product is soft and impressionistic, the disposition of the holes derives from a photograph of the trees along Jozenji Street. Abe's idea was to use the picture's precise distribution of light and dark spots to transfer the image of the trees onto his screen and bring the city inside.

The first step entailed dividing the tree photo into four grades of darkness and assigning each one a different-sized hole. Measuring 9 mm (0.35 in) in diameter, the largest holes represent the lightest areas and solid surface represents the darkest. Holes measuring 4 mm (0.16 in) and 6 mm (0.24 in) in diameter correspond to the shades between the two extremes. To geometrically order this organic distribution of light and dark, the dots were laid out on a 15 cm (6 in) grid, measured centre point to centre point.

The next challenge was finding a steel manufacturer able to perforate the 0.91 x 1.83 m (3 x 6 ft) steel panels and put them together with the required precision. This discounted standard architectural suppliers who handle large beams and hefty slabs. Instead, Abe turned to a shipbuilder who used a pneumatic drill to puncture the 2.3 mm (0.09 in) thick metal sheets and then welded them together at the factory. Just as was hoped, the steel shell was as seamless and self-supporting as the body of 'a Formula One racing car', as Abe puts it. The only problem was that the assemblage was too big to fit through the base building's doors.

This left no choice but to cut and re-weld the panels on site. Fortunately, a coat of matt paint embedded with high-tech ceramic powder rendered the seams practically invisible, and low-tech blow-torches were used to smooth out any warping. Slender tie rods to secure the steel form to the base building were the only necessary external elements.

Keeping the plenum behind the screen free of impediments was essential since Abe intended to light the room with 380 25-watt incandescent lamps attached to the screen's back. Basically, the whole space is lit by the walls. Filling the room with a mysterious, muted luminescence, the shimmering screen replicates the shadowy quality of light experienced while walking among the trees.

Though atmospheric, the diffuse light was insufficient for certain practical functions. Countering the deficit without compromising the original intention, stair treads are individually lit and the screen was cut in strategic places for the 50-watt pin lights that shine down on the dining tables and enable patrons to see their food.

Like the lacy screen, each Cow Table and accompanying Calf Chair that Abe created for Aoba-tei is an object formed from a single surface, this time moulded beech wood instead of steel. Bovine in stature and shape, the tables consist of a flat, 30 mm (1.18 in) thick eating surface that bends and turns into legs at either end. By contrast, the counter is a sculpted hunk of walnut wood whose extruded section remains the same all along its length but varies in height, delineating its separate functional areas.

Abe's comprehensive approach to the Aoba-tei interior blurs the boundary between architecture and furniture design. The counter is as much an architectural component as the delicate screen with its tiny lights is a furnishing. This approach is what enabled the architect to transform a mundane space into a place with a magical character all its own.

View from street

Aoba-tei   Ground-floor reception area

View from counter

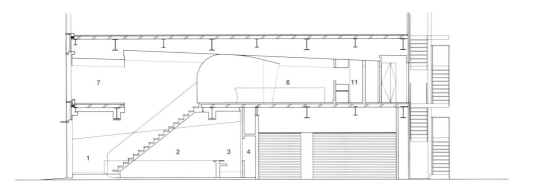

Section

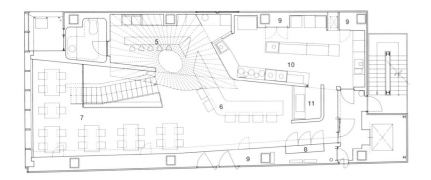

First-floor plan

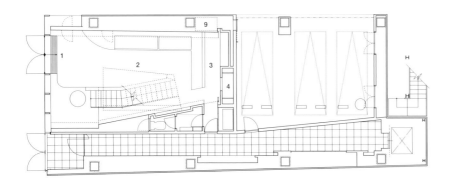

Ground-floor plan

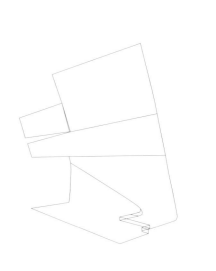

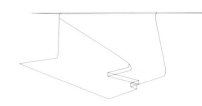

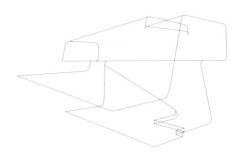

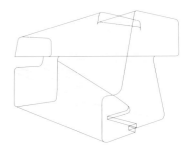

1	Entrance	7	Dining area
2	Hall	8	Wine cellar
3	Reception	9	Equipment
4	Cloakroom	10	Kitchen
5	Waiting bar (high stools)	11	Grill
6	Bar (chairs)		

Conceptual diagrams

0   5

Counter (top), view at top of stairs (bottom)

Aoba-tei

Main dining area with Cow Tables and Calf Chairs

Tokyo House KADO 001 [NHB]
Shibuya, Tokyo, Japan, 2005

In central Tokyo, where land values are among the world's highest, tiny properties and awkward plots abound. The direct result of landowners dividing their holdings into as many lots as possible, these oddly shaped, compact parcels saddled with setback restrictions can be a challenge to homeowners and architects alike. But to Yasuyuki Okazaki, an entrepreneur who markets architect-designed houses on the Internet, these severe conditions spelled opportunity. His second foray into drag-and-drop houses, Okazaki's 'Tokyo House' project identified three of the city's most awkwardly shaped site types – the flag-shaped site, the narrow eel's-nest site and the compact corner site – and commissioned an architect to create a generic solution for each one. All three architects devised a basic site strategy and a set of design guidelines for their appointed house type. For Abe, who authored the corner lot prototype, it did not take long for the first order to arrive. Okazaki liked his idea so much that he bought land, built the house and moved in with his family when construction finished in 2005.

The intention of the Tokyo House project was also to question Japan's ubiquitous nLDK house plan composed of a combined living room/dining room/kitchen plus a variable quantity of individual bedrooms. Popularized after World War II, this method, which emphasizes the number of rooms instead of the quality of the space, remains widely used. But according to Okazaki, 'more rooms do not equal more happiness. More volume does.' Elaborating on this sentiment, each model is a variant form of one-room living.

For the typically cramped corner-site house hemmed in by neighbours on two sides, Abe outlined very explicit rules for massing, floor plans and window placement. His objective was to make the most of the available land and bring in daylight from above – often the only sure source for crowded urban sites. He started by putting the bed and bathrooms on the lower level and the living, dining and kitchen areas in a continuous space above. Contained within a single tall volume divided into a series of stepped planes, the main living area is capped with a steep roof that slants from south to north. To limit exposure Abe wrapped the house with white walls, kept exterior openings to a minimum and put them either above or below, but not at, the eye level of passers-by.

Outside, the pitched roof complies with the so-called 'sunshine laws' governing the amount of shadow a new building can cast on its surroundings. Inside, the sloped ceiling bounces light from a south-facing clerestory window down into the room. The high opening works in tandem with a second window on the north wall. The external view at either end connects to nature, extends the space and challenges the sense of smallness within the house. In addition, operable panes on either side are intended to draw fresh air through the house. Within the confines of this system certain elements, including the front door, can be placed freely. 'It's like ordering a car,' explains Abe. 'There's the basic model and then a number of options to choose from.'

Located in a densely populated neighbourhood in the heart of Tokyo, the home occupies a 72 m^2 (775 sq ft) site bounded by a flag-shaped property on two sides and a narrow road barely wide enough for a car to pass in front. Though a parking space buffers the house from the street, mere centimetres separate it from the adjacent dwellings. The facade is a blank white wall whose smooth surface is broken only by the front door and a louvre-covered basement-level window. Abe's aim was to provide an honest response to what was there. Though the plain wrapping masks the house's inner workings, the roof's razor-sharp profile and the pure white walls stand out from the crowded surroundings.

Within the house, the exterior concrete stairs leading up to the front door level off and terminate in the foyer. From the entry hall, stairs go down to the private quarters or up to the modest sitting area – a small space embedded within a much bigger one. More home theatre than living room, it is lined with dark brown wood panels and built-in cabinetry concealing storage and a large flat-screen television set. Its low ceiling is devoid of light fixtures but contains six speakers. The entertainment area abuts the combined kitchen and dining area, where the slanted ceiling starts low but soars to 7 m (23 ft) on the south side. 'You can't actually have a big space in a Japanese house like this,' explains Abe. 'But you can have one that feels big.' Family life centres around this airy, open space defined by its rosewood floor, stained plywood cabinetry, combined with built-in appliances along its perimeter, and a large beechwood table in the middle. A stretched-out version of the tables Abe designed for his Aoba-tei restaurant in Sendai, the table is so long that its owners can eat at one end and work at the other.

From there, stairs ascend to the mezzanine which could be partially closed off as a second bedroom in the future by inserting three-quarter-height book shelves that will not block the flow of light from overhead. A ladder leads up to an 80 cm (32 in) wide catwalk. Bathed in sunlight from the clerestory, the steel-floored platform is ideal for clothes drying – a south-facing spot to hang laundry is uniformly coveted by homeowners in Japan. At the same time it acts like a mirror, directing sunlight back up to the ceiling.

Coated with glossy paint and unbroken by light or other surface-mounted fixtures, the slanted, 38-degree ceiling gives the main room its distinctive character. Its height creates spaciousness and its reflective surface bathes the room with soft, natural light whose colour changes slightly over the course of the day. On the other side of the room an expansive picture window lets in muted north light and overlooks the property next door. Though Okazaki's site is slightly higher than his neighbour's, the difference is not enough to shield his kitchen from view. But Okazaki accepts this situation. 'We don't care if they can see us,' says Okazaki. 'We live in Tokyo. It is inevitable.'

Encased in concrete, the lower level is completely closed to the surroundings. A structural hybrid, the house is supported by a wooden frame upstairs but reinforced concrete downstairs. Though both levels consist of continuous space, they are divided programmatically. Unlike upstairs, the private area – a study and a bedroom that may be partitioned by a folding wooden wall – is cosy and intimate. Clad with dark wooden walls and floor, the bedroom contrasts with the white-tiled bathroom. For efficiency's sake, Abe treated each of its fixtures as separate but connected entities that may be used independently. While the glass-enclosed bath area can be closed off with a roll screen, the lavatory can be hidden behind a pocket door.

In Japan, where a major proportion of the population lives in the so-called 'housemaker' houses designed and built by specialized contractors, the idea of ready-made design is not foreign. But the independently built Tokyo House projects are not completely congruent with the mass-produced domiciles. Instead of forcing an existing model into difficult site conditions Abe's Tokyo House tackles those constraints head on and uses them as design springboards. The end product is a house that is generic in its concept but uniquely suited to its site.

Entrance facade

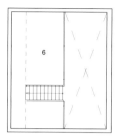

First-floor plan

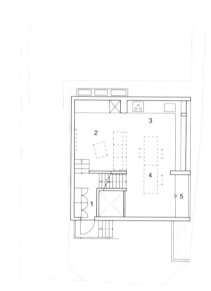

Ground-floor plan

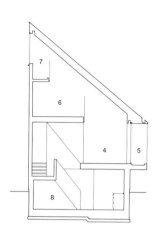

Section

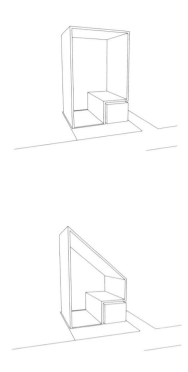

Conceptual diagrams

Basement-floor plan

1	Entrance	6	Interior terrace
2	Living room	7	Catwalk
3	Kitchen	8	Study room
4	Dining room	9	Main bedroom
5	Exterior terrace	10	Storage

View to the north (top), north facade (bottom left),
main entrance (bottom right)

Dining and living rooms with mezzanine terrace and
catwalk beyond

Tokyo House KADO 001

Stair to mezzanine terrace (top),
main bedroom (bottom)

Ceiling reflecting the colour of the sky (top), mezzanine terrace with catwalk above (bottom)

9 Tsubo House TALL [TH9]
Chigasaki, Kanagawa Prefecture, Japan, 2005

Ordering coffee used to boil down to choosing milk or sugar, but today's options go way beyond the basic brew. Like a contemporary coffee-bar menu, the website for the 9 Tsubo House brand of pre-designed homes serves up nine different versions of the Minimum House created by architect Makoto Masuzawa in 1952. Each one is a young architect's contemporary interpretation of Masuzawa's elegant but economic scheme. Intending to loosen up its compact prototype, Abe devised a tall-sized version of Masuzawa's short-sized original.

Constructed after World War II but before Japan's economic growth spurt in the 1960s, Masuzawa's Minimum House was realized at a time when land was cheap, but few had the means to build anything more than the most basic of homes. In designing the 50 m^2 (538 sq ft), two-storey dwelling with a double-height glass facade for his family, he hoped to reach a larger audience by setting higher design standards for low-cost houses.

Forty years later, as land prices grew and property sizes shrank, Masuzawa's ideas became particularly relevant once again. Featured in a Tokyo exhibition in 1999, the little house captivated a gallery-goer who found it so appealing that he decided to build one of his own. He enlisted the aid of architect Makoto Koizumi who adapted the prototype for a parcel in suburban Tokyo. Like the original, the completed house had a nine *tsubo*, or 29 m^2 (314 sq ft), footprint, hence the name. (A *tsubo* is a commonly used measurement of land in Japan, equivalent to 3.33 m^2 or 35.8 sq ft.)

In turn, Koizumi's 9 Tsubo House caught the attention of Yasuyuki Okazaki, an architect-turned-businessman who dreamed of selling house designs online. Okazaki saw an idea with mass appeal and a format well suited to Internet commerce. And by engaging the services of several architects, he saw a way to increase consumer options and satisfy a broader range of tastes. The project's idea was to give each architect free reign within the limitations of design tenets extrapolated from the Masuzawa original. Specifically, every house had to include three of the following: a square floor plan, a 3 *tsubo*/107 sq ft double-height space, an overall cubic form capped by a gabled roof, round columns, or a large south-facing window.

Using Masuzawa's Modernist ideals, Abe generated an entirely new house type tailored to the contemporary mindset. 'The original house was a compact, efficient box that decided how people live,' he explains. Today, according to Abe, there is a greater need for lifestyle flexibility. He met his goal by preserving the footprint of the original house but stretching its volume vertically and diffusing its directionality with four windowed walls instead of one dominant facade.

Based on Abe's schematic design, the client placed his online order. The purchase included a set of drawings plus support from Okazaki's and Abe's staff members, who modified the generic model to fit the client's particular needs and site. From there, the job was competitively bid and built just like any other.

Completed in 2005, the house is in a Tokyo suburb on a quiet cul-de-sac, surrounded by 'housemaker' homes, Japan's enormously popular dwellings that are designed, built and maintained by a single contractor. Once part of a large agricultural tract of land, today the site backs onto a veterinary clinic and abuts a large parking lot ripe for development. Though Abe's pitched roof and symmetrically shaped facades blend comfortably with the neighbouring

buildings adorned with white trim and mini-lawns, the house's tall proportions and chessboard wrapping imply that this is no garden-variety suburban bungalow.

'I don't like a facade that creates an image or an icon for a building,' says Abe. Unlike Masuzawa, Abe provided 18 full-height openings and distributed them evenly on his building's four faces. This equal treatment results in a generic solution independent of surrounding site conditions that are bound to change over time. As opposed to solid walls with punched windows, each facade is a balanced composition of opaque steel – coated with black, mocha or latté-coloured paint – and glass panels.

Since each side of the building is the same length, Abe could have arranged the panels in a uniform grid, though he chose not to. 'By changing its interval a grid can reveal different conditions happening behind.' Measuring 5.4 m (18 ft) on each side, the footprint divides into nine 1.8 x 1.8 m (6 x 6 ft) squares. But the bathroom's space requirements were too big to fit neatly inside this matrix and the entrance's were too small. Though they appear to be symmetrical and an even balance of solid and void, the chessboard walls' horizontal divisions reflect these subtle plan deviations and the floor levels determined the vertical dimensions of each glass pane. The only concessions to site conditions were the placement of balconies and the front door.

Replacing a ground-level glass panel, the front door is marked by a thin metal canopy. It leads directly into an open space filling half of the ground floor and functions as a combined entry foyer, play room and study. The other half holds the bathroom and an intimate Japanese-style room hidden from the outside by *shoji* paper screens and by sliding wood doors on the inside. Sleeping quarters for the family of three, this tatami-floored room is covered with nine removable square mats concealing a shallow storage area below. At night the mats are covered with futon folding mattresses.

Upstairs is the combined living/dining room and kitchen. It is a bright, airy room filled with natural light and cross-breezes from all directions, devoid of fixed elements aside from the kitchen's cooking area and free-standing counter. Instead of embedding a double-height space in his house as prescribed by the design guidelines, Abe's entire wood-covered first floor is a two-storey space. Strong enough to hold another floor, a pinwheel of wood beams divides the room vertically. Taking advantage of this support system, the clients added a small, ladder-accessible loft – a simple handrail-enclosed platform that can become a second sleeping or office area. ('The client clearly understood my idea of "possibility",' says Abe.) Windowed openings at floor and loft levels comply with Abe's overall facade strategy but also anticipate second-floor expansion. Together, the high windows and the pitched ceiling rising to 5.3 m (17 ft) at its apex draw attention up and away from the modest floor area.

Abe incorporated – but did not quote verbatim – the three requisite design tenets. Yet when it came to interior materials and details, he drew directly from Koizumi's palette of traditional-style *gettoshi* paper and bleached basswood veneer. 'In contrast to the sharp, white exterior I knew the interior spaces should be soft beige,' says Abe, who covered the house's inner lining with the surface-mounted paper. Objects placed within this shell, such as built-in closets and cabinetry or even the Japanese-style room, are defined by the whitish wood veneer. For hardware and furniture Abe turned again to Koizumi, who designs everyday objects that combine a clean, modern aesthetic with Japanese spatial sensibilities.

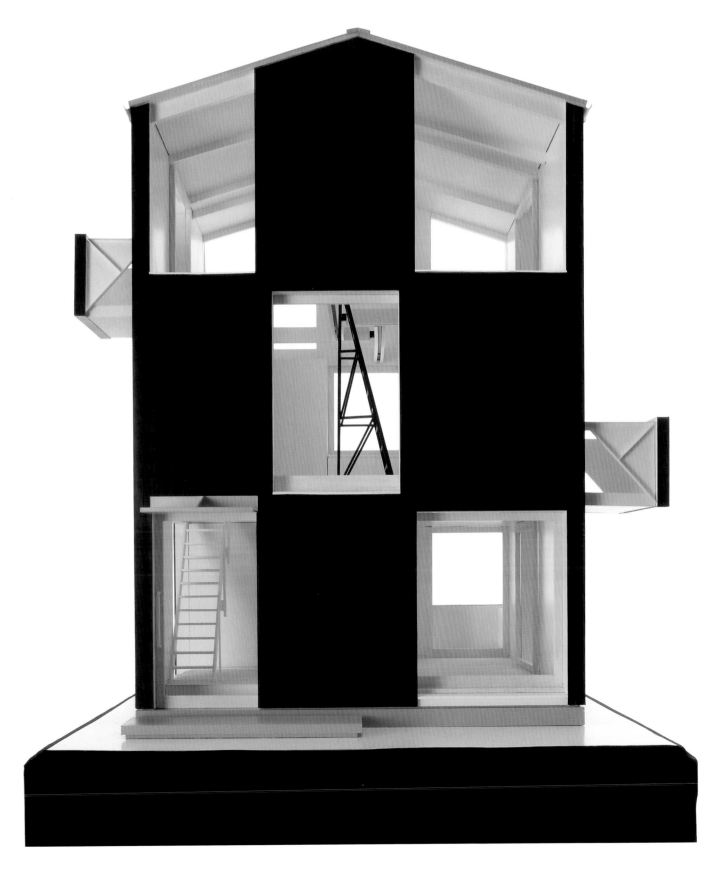

Study model

Loft-floor plan

First-floor plan

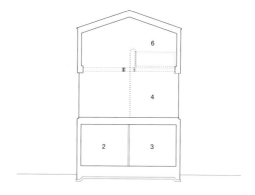

Section

Conceptual diagrams

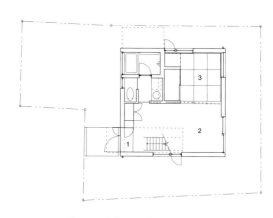

Ground-floor plan

1 Entrance
2 Workspace
3 Japanese-style room
4 Living/dining room
5 Kitchen
6 Loft

Entrance facade

9 Tsubo House TALL

View into kitchen

Workspace (top), living/dining room (bottom)

PTI and PTK
Sendai, Miyagi Prefecture, Japan, 2003 & 2005

Indisputably, Japan has produced some of the most spare, elegant architecture in the world. But it also invented the pachinko parlour – one of the most garish building types imaginable. Castles of neon crowned with show-stopping signage, these entertainment arcades jangle the nerves, jolt the eye and lure customers inside where seemingly endless rows of electronic games provide even more sensory overload. Clad with blinking lights, these pinball-like machines fill the interior with a deafening noise as they filter the thousands of tiny metal balls fed by gamblers hoping to win big. Though architects rarely have the opportunity to try their hands at pachinko parlour design, Abe has worked on two of them, both for the same client and both on the outskirts of Sendai.

First came PTI. This job, a facelift and interior renovation of an existing parlour topped by a six-storey parking garage, called for an attention-grabbing facade and the simplification of the original parlour's convoluted layout. In response, Abe devised a doughnut-shaped plan that placed the pachinko machines in the middle of the single-storey space and support functions around its perimeter. But the architect's boldest moves were on the outside, where he encircled the building base with a 100 m (328 ft) long curved facade intended to attract potential pachinko players cruising along the multi-lane thoroughfare in front. On top of that he capped the roof with a brash, drum-shaped, red neon sign visible from every direction.

Designed concurrently with the Sasaki Office Factory for Prosthetics, the artificial-limb factory enclosed with a concrete chessboard wrapping, the PTI facade is also composed of alternating void spaces and solid blocks – this time a surface-mounted screen of anodized aluminium panels. While the square panel size remained a constant 46 x 46 cm (18 x 18 in) from one end of the wall to the other, the intervals between them varied, yielding a pattern within the pattern. Where the spacing increases the subtle suggestion of a circle, an abstract reference to a pachinko ball emerges: especially at night when the panels, which are lit from behind, recede and the gap spaces become more visually prominent.

In his scheme for PTK, Abe once again knew that he had to come up with a striking facade that could literally stop traffic and convince car-bound customers to park and play. Unlike at PTI, this time Abe had a little more leeway since he was commissioned to design a brand-new, five-storey building. Even so, it was 'basically a decorated shed', according to the architect.

Though situated in the middle of a vast parking lot where the site constraints were few and far between, the building itself was saddled with numerous limitations and predetermined features. For starters the functional layout – multi-level parking on top and a single-storey parlour at grade – was a given. This fundamental decision by the client had a number of implications for Abe's scheme. Principally the garage needed a hefty steel structural system that impacted the size and determined the position of sturdy square columns below. In addition, the sequenced ramps required for vehicle access to the ascending parking levels left a sloped underside in their wake.

Abe could have masked the angled planes but instead he incorporated them into the ceiling over the parlour's perimeter zone containing support functions such as the prize display area, lounges, an Internet café, and the four parlour entrances marking the corners of the building's square plan. As in PTI, the heart of the building holds the pachinko machines – all 700 of them. In keeping with the client's wishes, Abe could not impair the visual connection between the two areas with walls or partitions.

Instead, lighting, colour schemes and ceiling heights distinguish the two areas. The outer zone is a series of distinct functions defined by white walls, brilliantly coloured furnishings and bright lights as well as the dynamic, sloped ceiling. By contrast, linear, double-loaded rows of pachinko machines comprise the building core, a 1,029 m² (11,076 sq ft) space with a dropped ceiling, dim lighting and dark furnishings designed to minimize distractions and maximize the drama of the game. A static space by comparison, here the only movement is the subtle flick of the wrist that separates winners from losers.

In true pachinko parlour style, the facade had to demand attention. Instead of resorting to applied signage or statuary, Abe envisioned the entire 60 m (197 ft) long surface as a giant billboard and uniformly covered it with a screen of perforated aluminium panels created in collaboration with the graphic designer Asao Tokolo. Each panel measures 100 cm (3 ft) square and has the same set of arc-shaped perforations. But arranging them in different combinations yielded a variety of motifs that segue seamlessly from one to the other like an optical illusion. The resultant circular and wave-like formations suggest the movement of pachinko's steel balls. While these transformations are clearly visible at night when the panels are lit from behind, they are their most dazzling at midday when the dotted screen casts a shadow on the solid masonry wall behind, resulting in a mind-boggling moiré effect.

In the recent past, pachinko – a legal form of gambling – had a somewhat unsavoury image and a limited clientele, though today it is practically family entertainment. Intended to appeal to a broader audience, these designer versions satisfy the typology's need for eye-popping exterior expression but in a sophisticated way.

PTK facade detail

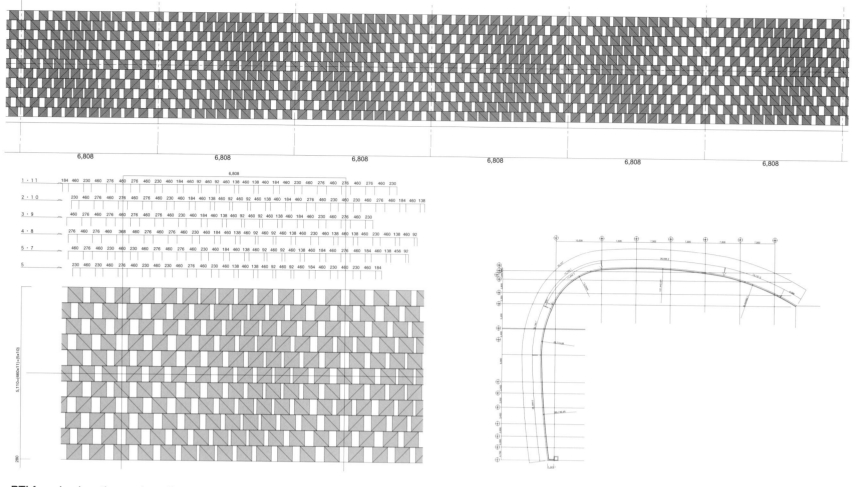

6,808   6,808   6,808   6,808   6,808   6,808

1·11   184 460 230 460 276 460 276 460 230 460 184 460 92 460 138 460 184 460 230 460 276 460 276 460 276 460 230

2·10   230 460 276 460 276 460 276 460 230 460 184 460 138 460 92 460 92 460 138 460 184 460 276 460 276 460 230 460 230 460 276 460 184 460 138

3·9   460 276 460 276 460 276 460 276 460 230 460 184 460 138 460 92 460 92 460 138 460 184 460 230 460 276 460 230

4·8   276 460 276 460 368 460 276 460 276 460 230 460 184 460 138 460 92 460 138 460 184 460 138 460 230 460 184 460 138 460 92

5·7   460 276 460 230 460 230 460 276 460 276 460 230 460 184 460 138 460 92 460 138 460 184 460 230 460 184 460 456 92

5   230 460 230 460 276 460 230 460 276 460 230 460 184 460 138 460 92 460 92 460 138 460 184 460 230 460 230 460 184

5,110=(460x11)=(5x10)

280

PTI facade elevation and section

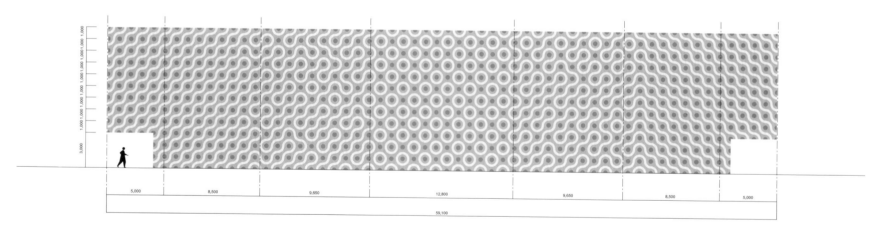

1,000 1,000 1,000 1,000 1,000 1,000 1,000 1,000

3,000

5,000   8,500   9,650   12,800   9,650   8,500   5,000

59,100

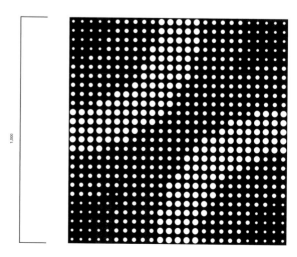

1,000

PTK facade elevation and detail

PTI facade (top), facade detail (bottom)

PTK facade by day (top) and night (bottom)

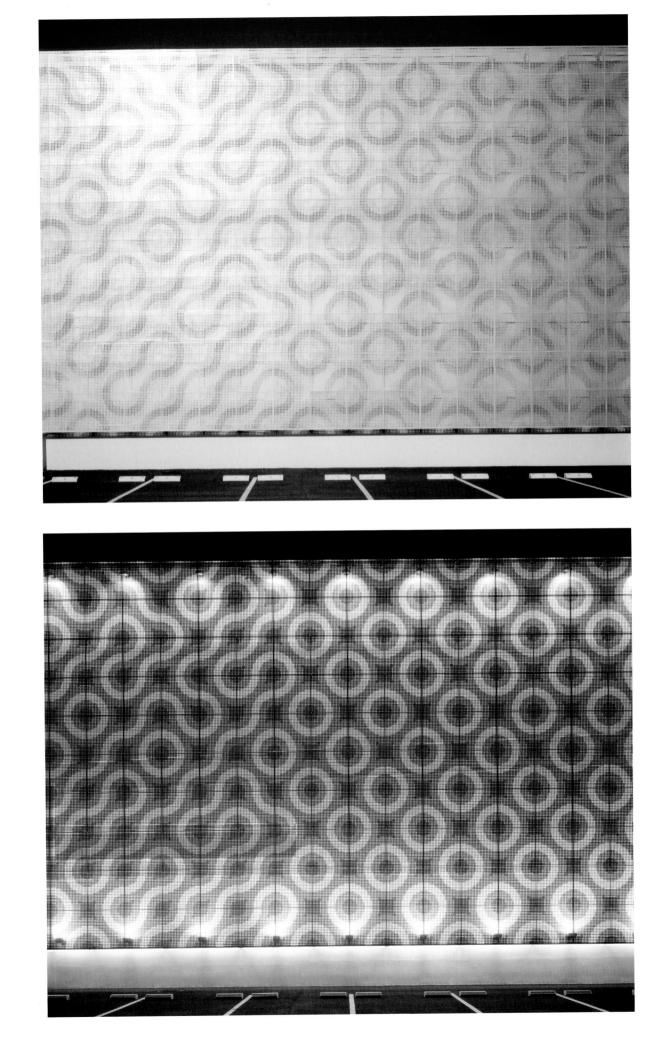

PTK facade detail by day (top) and night (bottom)

Dining Dayu [DIP]
Sendai, Miyagi Prefecture, Japan, 2003

In Japan, where people have an insatiable appetite for eating and drinking outside their homes, countless tiny bars and cafés fill city streets and multi-storey restaurant buildings. Since they combine social and culinary experiences, these eating establishments must provide more than good food to keep hungry diners coming back for more – snappy interior design and a trendy image are often essential ingredients for success. But keeping up with the competition requires restaurateurs to routinely renovate their spaces. Abe's redesign of Dayu, a casual diner frequented by young people, was completed in 2003.

Occupying the first floor of a typical, six-storey, reinforced concrete restaurant tower on one of Sendai's busiest commercial streets, the existing bar was divided into many separate rooms connected by a complicated circulatory system. But the client wanted to host wedding parties and large events in addition to small gatherings. With this goal in mind Abe concluded that multiple seating areas that could be converted into one large space was the answer.

Achieving this flexibility first required getting rid of all unnecessary internal walls. Working around lavatories, air-conditioning ducts, fire safety elements and other fixed pieces, Abe blanketed the base building's concrete walls with an inner skin made of wood. Composed of 90 cm (3 ft) wide by 285 cm (9 ft) tall panels, the semi-permeable membrane doubled as a movable screen system. This approach enabled the proprietor to partition the interior in various ways, simply by sliding the panels along a ceiling-mounted track and bolting them to the floor while still allowing light and sound to travel. And when not in use as dividers, the screens could be flattened against the perimeter walls to transform the 201 m² (2,164 sq ft) space into one room.

Composed of vertical bars spanned by short, staggered horizontal blocks of reddish cedar, the panels' elongated chessboard pattern was an expressive decorative motif that provided visual texture and colour to the otherwise neutral interior. Made of concrete coated with clear epoxy paint, the floor is enlivened with shadows cast by the free-standing screens' 30 by 120 mm (1 by 5 in) openings. When the screens are folded back, many of these little openings frame display niches built into the existing walls. Though just big enough for a single flower or small object, collectively these tiny individual alcoves made a dramatic impact.

Though the base building remains standing, Abe's interior design, like many eateries of a similar ilk, had a limited shelf life from the start. Like the miniature displays that could be easily rotated, the restaurant itself has already changed hands.

Steel doors dividing casual dining spaces

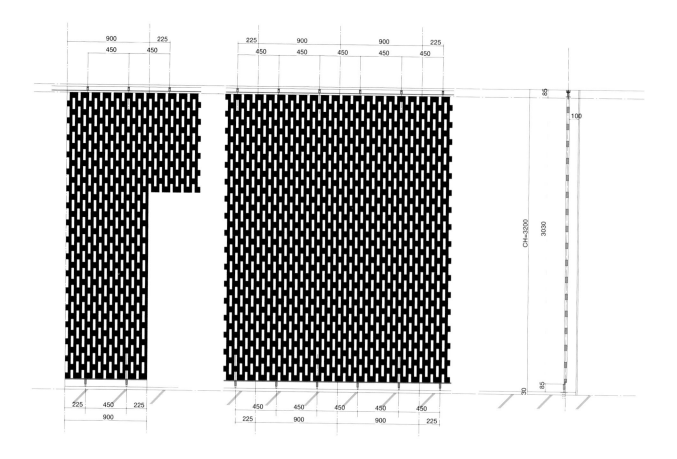

Screen detail

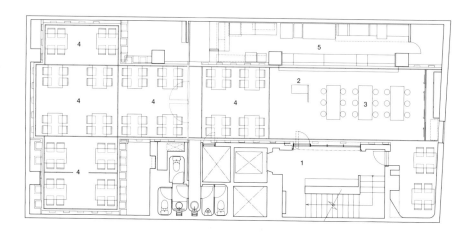

Floor plan

1 Entrance hall
2 Reception
3 Dining space (casual)
4 Dining space (formal)
5 Kitchen

0   5

Dining area, two views

Dining Dayu

Detail, chessboard screen

VOLUME

Volume

In Japan, where sites can be tight and legal restrictions limiting, many designers begin by calculating the permissible building volume and then work inwards. Out of necessity, this was the approach Abe used in his design for Gravel 2, a three-generation home that fills its sliver-like site to legal capacity. In his scheme for the modest private home, JB-House, Abe adopted a similar strategy by starting with a solid block and paring away bits and pieces to intersperse interior and exterior spaces. For other residential works, such as M-House and Whopper, Abe added volumetric blocks together to address the clients' requests, while responding to site conditions such as adjacent buildings and busy roads. For the two clinics, Sekii Ladies Clinic and M-Dental Clinic, Abe divided the programme into two volumes and then placed one on top of the other, separating functions and creating dramatic, top-heavy buildings for each one. Like JB-House and Y-House, the perimeters of both medical facilities incorporate small gardens that simultaneously connect the interior to and separate it from its surroundings. Using three-dimensional space as a buffer results in a boundary that is both ambiguous and sharply defined.

The private Kanno Museum marks a new direction for Abe. A simple steel box on the outside, it contains a pile of bubble-like rooms that press against each other. Instead of clear-cut floor levels and uniform ceiling heights, the top of one bubble is also the bottom or side of its neighbour. In a similar but less sculptural vein, the eat-and-drink building F-town was conceived as a stack of six two-storey cubes interspersed with void spaces. Abutting each other at different levels, the cubes' interiors can be combined in different ways by the building tenants.

Kanno Museum, Shiogama, Miyagi Prefecture, 2005.
Study model. →

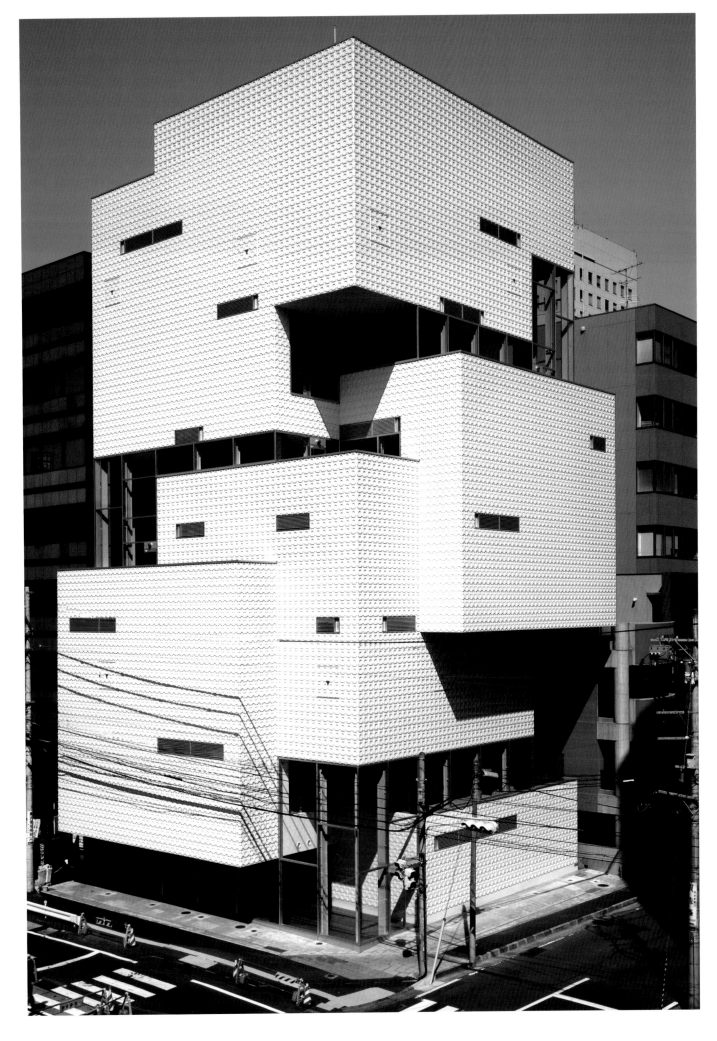

F-town, Sendai, Miyagi Prefecture, 2007. Exterior view.

Gravel 2 [G2P]
Sendai, Miyagi Prefecture, Japan, 1998

To promote the development of Ayashi, a new suburb 5 km (3 miles) west of downtown Sendai, a pioneering real-estate mogul decided the best way was to live there himself. At the time the residential enclave was little more than a collection of vacant lots bounded by a street grid. Out of the available sites he selected a corner plot and hired Abe to design a three-generation home where he could live under the same roof as his parents, his wife and their three children. But this was no ordinary piece of land. Though a respectable 25 m (82 ft) long, it measured a mere 5 m (16 ft) across at its highly valued southern end. 'It wasn't much wider than a pedestrian sidewalk,' jokes Abe.

Instead of grappling directly with this harsh reality, Abe formed his conceptual foothold by idealizing the awkward parcel. First, he turned the lot's extreme geometry into a well-proportioned rectangle and reoriented it towards the south. Next, he created the perfect house for the now perfect property. It consisted of three solid volumes: one for the grandparents, one for the communal spaces and one for the client and his wife.

But then Abe had to reverse the process and mould his model to the actual site conditions. This took the form of realigning the three blocks like railway carriages along the 150 m² (1,615 sq ft) site's north–south axis and interspersing them with two void spaces that articulate the volumes and ameliorate the problem of daylight access due to the property's meagre southern exposure. Because a busy street and an empty, construction-ready lot straddle the client's strip of land, this strategy also permitted oblique views out without compromising the family's privacy, even if a building goes up next door.

Hugging the house's east facade, an exterior corridor-like entrance ramp leads up from the south side street to the front door and entry alcove in the middle of the wooden framed house. The tallest and largest of the three volumes, the centre box holds a modest living room ringed with built-in seating and the combined dining room/kitchen, a sky lit, double-height space where the entire family congregates. Separated from this core by a small west-side courtyard, the grandparents' ground-floor quarters, a generous bedroom with private bathroom, fill the front of the house. A second courtyard carved into the east side distinguishes the kitchen's cooking area from the bathroom suite, the rear entrance and two off-street but outdoor parking spots beyond that. Upstairs are bedrooms for the client's daughter at the front of the house, one for each of his two sons above the living room and, connected by a bridge spanning the kitchen below, the master bedroom with its own private terrace just big enough for one. A second, roomier terrace, this one accessed by stairs up from the first floor's circulation spine, tops off the building.

Because of the site's dramatic dimensions and its proximate neighbours, allowing light in but keeping prying eyes out was a real balancing act. Instead of windows – there are some but most are screened with wooden louvres – the perimeter courtyards are the main vehicles for controlling visual contact between inside and out. Abe not only named the house after these two gravel-covered yards, but he also adapted them in his design of the Sekii Ladies Clinic. While their floor-to-ceiling glass panes let in some daylight, the primary source is a huge skylight above the kitchen. A 3.8 x 3.5 m (12 x 11 ft) sheet of glass reinforced with steel mesh, it bathes the heart of the house with light that permeates into the adjacent rooms.

To preserve the integrity of the three main volumes, Abe enclosed each one with solid walls of metal lath covered with mortar and then white, spray-on acrylic coating that imparts a slightly gritty texture to the otherwise smooth surfaces. By contrast, the interstitial volumes and areas related to openings were enclosed with horizontal bands of galvanized metal siding painted dark grey. But Abe was not a slave to geometry – neither dark nor light boxes are entirely pure forms. Instead they jut out in response to the plan inside, cut back to make room for exterior terraces and even nest together where the living room abuts the kitchen. Encased in black steel, external downspouts read as straight lines that add another layer of articulation and draw attention to the building's verticality. Though south facing, the windowless front facade is an artful composition of increasingly taller grey and white blocks that similarly draw the eye steadily upwards.

The emphasis on verticality came about partially in anticipation of the area's future development. But it was also Abe's way of coping with a very common condition in urban Japan – the tiny site. Because of the tremendous horizontal limitations, Abe expanded in the one direction he could. Adding a little grandeur and a much-needed sense of spaciousness, building upwards compensates for a small footprint and makes the best of a tight situation.

Front facade

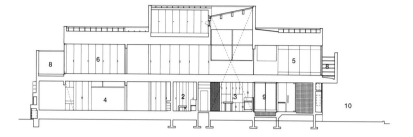

Section

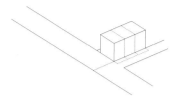

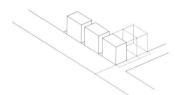

First-floor plan

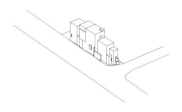

Conceptual diagrams

Ground-floor plan

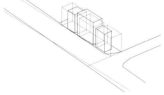

1	Entrance	6	Daughter's bedroom
2	Living room	7	Son's bedroom
3	Dining room/kitchen	8	Terrace
4	Grandparents' bedroom	9	Courtyard
5	Main bedroom	10	Parking

West facade (top), east facade (bottom)

Approach to master bedroom

First-floor corridor and sons' bedrooms

M-House [MH]
Haramachi, Fukushima Prefecture, Japan, 1999

In 1998, a developer asked Abe to devise a planned community prototype on the west side of Sendai. Eager to break away from the rows of small houses found in most Japanese suburbs, Abe proposed filling the 1,500 m² (16,146 sq ft) site with a chessboard of houses and gardens. Typically the house is placed on the site's north side and garden on the south, but Abe put each home in the middle of its lot and surrounded it with yards on all four sides. Instead of looking at the neighbour's back wall, gardens now faced gardens. By using greenery to bridge the gap between houses Abe hoped to promote good neighbourly relations yet maintain a comfortable distance between houses.

Collectively, the development's eight centripetally organized, residential lots appeared as a uniform solid and void pattern. Within this framework, however, there were many subtle variations generated by the design of the individual homes. Though Abe stipulated the same volumetric components for all houses – each one was composed of a large, square box with four attached smaller boxes – his system permitted a modicum of compositional flexibility. The appendages not only ranged in size – they could be affixed either on the central volume's orthogonal or diagonal axes. Though small gestures, these variations had a big impact on the overall site plan.

Unfortunately, this project was never realized. But when a friend's mother asked Abe to design her new home, the architect resurrected the individual unit concept. Her space needs were compatible with the developer prototype and her site was comparable in size as well as character. Her one request was that Abe build with wood. And preferably sugi (cedar) or hinoki (cypress). Having worked for a timber company, this was a client with strong preferences when it came to wood.

In other respects, the client was very flexible. Her site did not present any extreme conditions either. Located in a typical residential neighbourhood in Haramachi, at that time a town of 48,000 in Fukushima Prefecture, 74 km (46 miles) from Sendai, the 165 m² (1,776 sq ft), nearly square site faced a narrow road to the north and a parking lot to the south. M-House, a two-storey building with a cruciform plan, sits in the middle of this site. While the scale of the 100 m² (1,076 sq ft) home blended well with those of its neighbours, its sculptural assemblage of boxes made of dark wood and glass contrasted sharply with the compact, undifferentiated shape of the nearby homes.

The heart of the house is a large cubic volume whose ground floor holds the entrance foyer and the combined living/dining room. Projecting from each of the room's four sides is a small rectilinear room that juts out into the garden and increases the house's exterior exposure in every direction. The east box contains the kitchen, the west box a tatami-mat guest room, the north box holds the bathroom and lavatory and the south box stairs up to the first floor. Upstairs, the main volume is divided into two bedrooms, one Western-style and the other a tatami-floored, Japanese-style room opening onto a roof terrace atop the west-side box. Thanks to the division of space between the two floors, the client can easily convert to single-storey living if desired in the future.

Another benefit of Abe's protruding boxes is that they yielded four L-shaped yards, each one wrapped around a corner of the central volume but ear-marked for a different purpose. Abe envisioned one each for flowers, vegetables, parking and a Japanese landscape. But treating all sides of the house equally challenged the convention in Japan, where the southern exposure is maximized whenever possible and certainly not divided by a stair enclosure as it is here. At M-House, however, this wall faces asphalt and parked cars. Abe resolved the conflict between the ideal and the real site conditions with floor-to-ceiling glass that lets in plenty of sunlight on either side of the projection. And instead of compromising the view the box improves it by obliquely directing the gaze towards scenery that is more appealing. 'Looking out at an angle distances people inside from strangers outside,' explains Abe, who used walls and windows in a similar way at the Sekii Ladies Clinic.

As lots open up nearby, Abe hopes that M-House will act as a catalyst for new construction and that, bit by bit, his original site plan will be realized. Though this is unlikely to happen anytime soon, elements of Abe's chessboard plan resurfaced in his design for Arai Public Housing, a subsidized housing project built by the city of Sendai in 2004. A 50-unit apartment block interspersed with courtyards and covered parking, this project, like the developer prototype, relies on open spaces and outdoor greenery to unite people and build a sense of community.

View from garden

Section

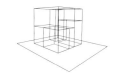

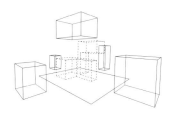

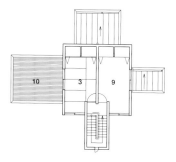

First-floor plan

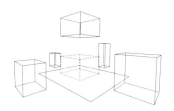

Conceptual diagrams

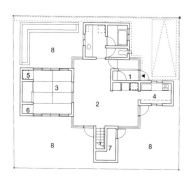

Ground-floor plan

1   Entrance
2   Living/dining room
3   Japanese-style room
4   Kitchen
5   Buddhist altar

6   Tokonoma
7   Storage
8   Garden
9   Western-style room
10 Roof deck

0   5

View from street (top), living room (bottom)

M-Dental Clinic [ADC]
Sendai, Miyagi Prefecture, Japan, 2001

In Japan, where pain is often tolerated instead of obliterated, a visit to the dentist is not always a benign experience. But a pleasant environment can certainly make treatment more palatable. With that goal in mind, the owner of M-Dental Clinic, a solo practitioner with a unique, holistic approach to oral hygiene, decided to build himself a new clinic in the recently developed Sendai suburb of Ayashi. Convinced that a series of private rooms would yield better care and a more positive outcome for his patients than the typical multi-chaired examination area, the dentist came to his initial meeting with Abe, drawing in hand. The dentist's idea immediately got Abe's creative juices flowing. 'We looked at his sketch and thought we could make a village of rooms, each one with its own character,' says the architect. Based on this concept, Abe sculpted a tripartite building composed of individuated boxes that neatly matches the long but narrow site.

Generously sized, the 987 m² (10,624 sq ft) site backs onto an empty lot and a busy road beyond that. In front, a spacious parking area separates the building from the street, a winding road barely wide enough for cars to make their way through the surrounding residential neighbourhood. Buffered by a line of newly planted trees along its south face, the 435 m² (4,682 sq ft) clinic fits snugly between rows of houses on either side. A privacy screen for the largely transparent south facade, the leafy trees let in daylight and provide seated patients with a view of nerve-calming greenery. By contrast, the north facade, like the entrance facade, is made mostly of 15 mm (0.5 in) thick unfinished, extruded cement board. Crowned by a top-heavy volume with a single rounded corner, the facade consists of three clearly articulated, square-shaped bays that correlate to the symmetrical plan.

The clinic's two front entrances, one for staff and one for patients, are located in the interstices on either side of the central bay. Both pass by the reception area, a double-height space infused with daylight from above, and feed into parallel circulation conduits that extend the length of the building. The twin hallways lead to a series of small, discrete rooms that line the building perimeter and contain the various treatment and consulting areas. Sandwiched between the two corridors, technical areas, such as the instrument sterilization and X-ray rooms, are equally accessible from either side. Off-setting the compartmentalized programme, skylights, glass partitions and a tiny interior garden create openness and fluidity throughout the entire ground floor. Even the sterilization room is enclosed with partial glass walls that allow light rays and sight lines to cross from one side to the other. By contrast, the first floor is encapsulated in a single monolithic volume containing a seminar room, doctors' offices, a locker room and other support functions.

Intended to unify all the disparate pieces below, the form of the first floor started out as a simple rectangular tube. But Abe found this boring, and in response rounded off three of its four edges – two on the bottom and one on top – resulting in the clinic's distinctive exterior profile. Painted dark grey, the asymmetrical element is oriented towards the south where its largely glass straight side lets in plenty of daylight. Flanked by strips of skylights set into the roof covering the ground floor, the volume's curved underside hovers independently over the warren of rooms below.

Downstairs, Abe used void spaces to isolate and articulate the cubic rooms. Separated by small courtyards, the boxes differ slightly in use and expression. Each one holds function-appropriate furnishings such as a single examination chair in the consulting rooms, a built-in counter plus sink in the toothbrushing room, worktables in the lab and tatami-mat flooring in the staff lounge. The showpiece of the collection is a floor-to-ceiling glass box that holds three treatment areas separated by free-standing, three-quarter-height frosted glass partitions. Designed in consultation with Alan Burden, a Tokyo-based structural engineer from Great Britain, the self-supporting transparent enclosure is made of two layers of laminated, tempered glass with a thin adhesive film in-between. While a steel frame ties the top edges of the glass together, a metal channel bonds them to the concrete foundation below.

Another contribution by the engineer was the clinic's unique structural system. For ease of construction the architect and his engineer agreed to build with lightweight steel angles that were bolted together on site to form cross-shaped beams. Though conventional beams often require the expertise of skilled steel manufacturers and the lifting power of heavy-duty cranes, the clinic's slender elements were easily carried by hand. Left largely exposed, the simple system melded nicely with Abe's additive composition.

In keeping with the client's down-to-earth approach to dental care, the clinic is modest and unpretentious. But beneath its understated wrapping is an airy, uplifting interior that is bound to put both patients and practitioners at ease.

Glass-enclosed examination room

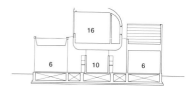

Sections

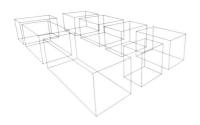

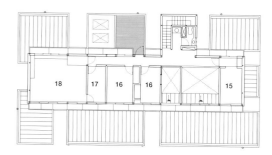

First-floor plan

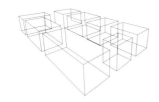

Conceptual diagrams

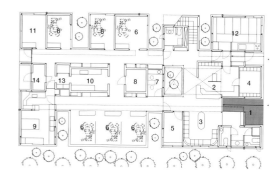

Ground-floor plan

1	Main entrance	10	Sterilization room
2	Reception	11	Examination room
3	Waiting room	12	Staff lounge
4	Archive	13	Storage
5	Consulting room	14	Mechanical room
6	Medical examination room	15	Locker
7	Toothbrushing room	16	Doctor's office
8	X-ray room	17	Chief doctor's office
9	Laboratory	18	Seminar room

0   10

Entrance facade (top), examination room (bottom)

M-Dental Clinic

Ground-floor circulation space

First-floor access (top left), ground-floor clinic space
(top right), reception area (bottom)

Sekii Ladies Clinic [FLC]
Osaki, Miyagi Prefecture, Japan, 2001

Bounded by car dealers, fast-food joints and garden supply stores, the site of Sekii Ladies Clinic hardly sounds suited to birthing babies. Yet, in spite of this, the roadside site in Osaki, a city just north of Sendai, appealed to a young, husband-and-wife doctor team eager to launch their maternity practice. Because the surrounding area was neither saturated with obstetrical clinics nor, thanks to its job-generating high-tech industry, in danger of succumbing to Japan's plummeting birthrate, the doctors felt confident that they would find enough patients. And the surrounding noise and neon, though far from desirable, could be tamed with Abe's architectural ingenuity.

After assessing the site conditions, Abe quickly surmised that his top priority had to be buffering his building from – yet maintaining a connection to – its car-oriented environment. Conventional solutions like walled gardens and generous setbacks were out of the question because of the extensive programme Abe had to squeeze into the site's modest 2,127 m² (22,895 sq ft) size. The architect could have designed an inwardly focused fortress but, instead, he proposed a 1,521 m² (16,372 sq ft) building that gradually retreats from the external chaos and culminates in a quiet inner sanctum.

Though comprised of many intricate pieces, the programme is conveniently divided into three related but discrete parts. Abe put the outpatient clinic on the ground floor, the 19-bed inpatient facility on the first and a three-generation home for the couple, their children and the client's mother and father at the rear of the property. This distanced the birthing centre from the street and concentrated the busy waiting areas and examination rooms on the ground floor close to the adjacent car park. But the levels did not stack up. 'After we added all the floor areas together we realized that the first floor would be much bigger than the ground floor,' says Abe. Instead of abandoning his plan, he accepted the top-heavy shape, and with surgical precision excised deep recesses, giving the building a unique crenulated profile.

The building fronts the road with a monolithic white box that appears to float above its glass base but is actually anchored by steel columns and cantilevered beams. Defining the building's central spine, the square pillars support 7.5 m (25 ft) long trussed beams that run cross-wise. They hold up the windowless white blocks comprising the first floor. Though the hospital's night entrance faces the street, its main portal is tucked beneath the massive eave-like projections on the west side, the building's de facto facade.

This doorway leads directly into the outpatient waiting area composed of two overlapping rectangular rooms. One includes the reception area, a double-height, skylit space open to the inpatient facility upstairs. The other leads to the heart of the clinic: its maze of examination and treatment rooms. A second set of doors restricts access to rest areas for the doctors and nurses, the hospital kitchen and storage rooms at the back of the building, where a private entrance goes directly outside and stairs and a dumb waiter connect to the first floor.

Bracketing the other end of the building's doughnut-shaped circulation, the main stairs and lift are located near the hospital entrance, providing direct access from the street to the inpatient birthing centre even when the clinic is closed. Hidden behind closed doors, the delivery suite and operating room are near the top of the stairs but completely cut off from the rest of the building. They share the floor's front end with a glass-enclosed nursery for newborn infants and a spacious lounge for proud parents and their visitors.

Accommodation for new mothers – in Japan, women typically spend a week in the hospital postpartum – occupies the rear of the first floor. A wide, windowed corridor, flanked by four-bed communal wards on one side and clusters of private rooms on the other, runs the length of the building. Interspersed between the staggered blocks of rooms, recesses and roof gardens enliven the conduit with natural light and oblique exterior views. Going against the grain of the street grid, the angled sight lines offer glimpses of but maintain clinical distance from the cars whizzing by below.

Upstairs, Abe avoided full-on street views by limiting glass and swaddling primary facades with bold, blank walls instead. One wall in the lounge has a floor-to-ceiling window that captures a sidelong view of moving vehicles. But the airy, table-filled space confronts the highway head on with a solid wall. The only opening is a long glass strip, well below eye level. 'It is more interesting to look down at cars than across at ugly buildings,' reasons the architect.

In the same vein, windowless end walls in the wards thwart abrupt views out and divert the gaze to artful arrangements of transparent and opaque panels on either side. The composite planes not only protect privacy and ensure a restful environment; they mask the building's underlying structure. 'I thought exposing the structural braces was too brutal in a maternity hospital,' says Abe. Instead he blanketed them with steel panels and inserted glass between their slanted limbs. Inside the rooms, the solid surfaces correlate with wood-clad closets and cabinetry and the glass panels frame fragmented views out.

A combination of smooth steel, corrugated spandrel plates oriented in two different directions and diagonally scored ceramic tile, the hospital's tough skin is pure white but not antiseptic. The various hues and textures catch and deflect light in multiple ways. Downstairs, by contrast, the exterior wrapper is almost completely see-through. Shielded by the overhanging first floor, the clinic is sheathed in 12 mm (0.5 in) thick, self-supporting, full-height glass coated with surface-mounted striped fritting that filters visibility. Filling out the plan's perimeter recessions, three tiny glass-enclosed gardens add another layer of protection that physically distances the clinic from the parking area and draws the eye towards patches of greenery instead.

Without missing a beat, a fourth garden continues the building's solid–void cadence but separates the doctors' residence and workplace. 'The whole idea was to fit five volumetric blocks into a very limited site,' says Abe. While proximity was a plus, the two-storey house is a self-contained entity painted grey to distinguish it from the hospital. Divided in section, it holds two interlocking but, aside from a shared entry hall, independent homes: the young couple and their children live upstairs while the client's parents occupy the downstairs unit, where their dog can play freely in the yard. To preserve privacy inside, Abe positioned the two master bedrooms and living rooms at opposite ends of their respective linear plans.

Completed in 2001, the Sekii Ladies Clinic is by no means the nation's first free-standing, privately owned women's healthcare facility. Nor is the attached residence a novelty. What is distinctive about Abe's building is its warm, welcoming character – in Japan, medical institutions tend towards the cold and clinical. Good design may not be able to increase the country's birth rate. But women who choose to have babies in Furukawa can at least do it in style and comfort.

Exterior recess

Sections

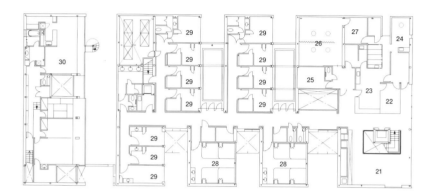

First-floor plan

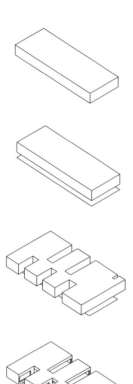

Conceptual diagrams

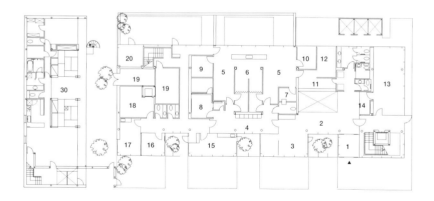

Ground-floor plan

1	Entrance	16	Meeting room
2	Waiting room	17	Staff lounge
3	Playroom	18	Kitchen
4	Inner waiting room	19	Storage
5	Consulting room	20	Mechanical room
6	Internal examination room	21	Lounge
7	Examination room 1	22	Newborn nursery
8	X-ray room	23	Nurse station
9	Sterilization room	24	Breast-feeding room
10	Examination room 2	25	Labour room
11	Reception desk	26	Delivery room
12	Archive	27	Preparation room
13	Multi-purpose room	28	Group bedroom
14	Locker room	29	Private bedroom
15	Doctor's office	30	Doctor's residence

0   5

Front facade (top), east facade (bottom)

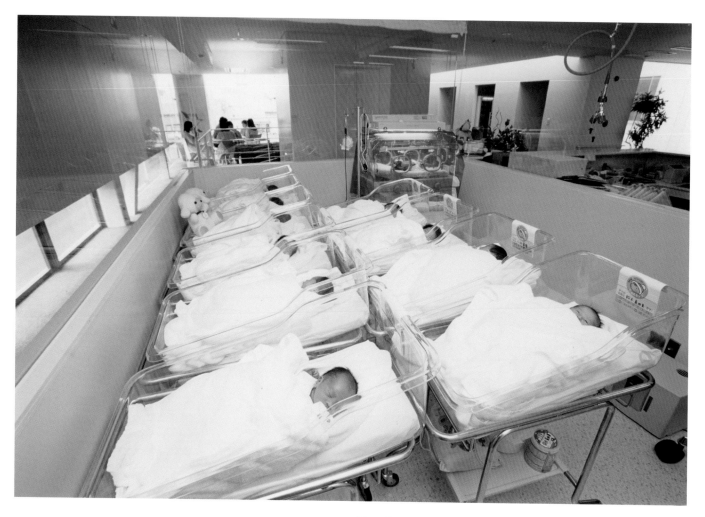

First-floor lounge (top left), private bedroom (top right),
newborn nursery (bottom)

Ground-floor waiting room

Y-House [YH]
Yamagata, Yamagata Prefecture, Japan, 2003

A streamlined, garage-like structure, Y-House was designed for a 'salariman' with a taste for fancy Italian cars. Replacing his family home, the new dwelling enables the client to live side-by-side with his parents while admiring his red Alfa Romeo. Occupying a place of honour within one of the house's perimeter courtyards, the classic sports car is visible from every room on his side of the house.

Located in a suburb of Yamagata, a city of 250,000 located 360 km (224 miles) north-east of Tokyo, the client's 1,478 m² (15,909 sq ft) site was large by Japanese standards, but his budget was small. To take advantage of the available land while keeping costs down, Abe proposed a single-storey building. Throughout the house the ceiling height is a modest 2.35 m (8 ft), but the plan compensates by expanding horizontally.

Embedded on the south side of the oblong, 228 m² (2,454 sq ft) house, a courtyard leads to the main entrance. Located in the middle of the building, the foyer opens into the communal zone – it contains a large living/dining room, kitchen and a bathroom – where the two generations overlap. While the parents' quarters, a bedroom and large tatami-floored guest room, complete with a *tokonoma* decorative alcove, fill the house's west end, the study, bedroom and separate living/dining room with a built-in kitchenette belonging to their son and his wife fill the east.

Reminiscent of many traditional Japanese homes, the individual rooms are interspersed with exterior courtyards – six in total. Basically, the courtyards articulate the functions. Enclosed with floor-to-ceiling glass on three sides, the gravel-covered outdoor rooms clearly distance the house's interior spaces but simultaneously link them back together visually. 'We like the way you can see through the courtyards,' says Abe. 'Instead of high ceilings we have a layered plan.'

Unlike the fluidity of the inside space, the division between the rectangular building and its site is very explicit. Similar to historic *naka niwa*, all of Abe's gardens (except for the Alfa Romeo's covered space) are open to the sky and infuse the interior with soft daylight. But unlike their precedents, these contemporary renditions are not included within the house. Like the courtyards Abe designed for the Sekii Ladies Clinic, Gravel 2 and other projects, they are located at the building perimeter. Yet they are not fully fused with the site either. Since the client disliked the view from his house, he asked the architect to shut it out. But Abe did not want to seal off the house and sever ties to the outdoors. As a compromise, he installed fixed panels of metal fins at the outer edges of the courtyards that impede sight lines without blocking them entirely.

Painted gunmetal grey, the slatted, fixed louvres add texture to the lightweight concrete panels comprising the exterior walls. Secured by a simple wooden-frame structure, the house was laid out using the traditional Japanese measurement system derived from the dimensions of a tatami mat. This module makes it easy to describe the size of a room to clients and contractors.

Against the backdrop of the building's monochrome material palette, the car's cherry-red chassis really stands out. Surely this is no coincidence. 'The client treats this car like a sculpture,' says Abe. Thanks to Abe's design, the owner never has to take his eyes off it.

View through living room

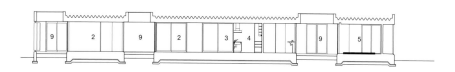

Section

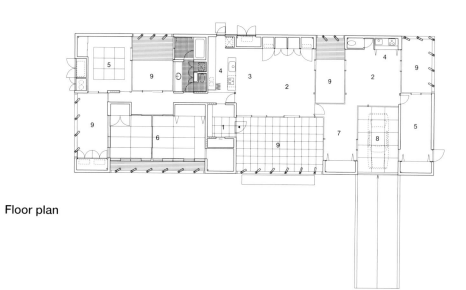

Floor plan

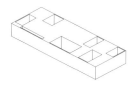

Conceptual diagrams

1	Entrance	6	Japanese-style room
2	Living room	7	Study room
3	Dining room	8	Garage
4	Kitchen	9	Courtyard
5	Bedroom	10	Terrace

0   5

Facade detail (top), exterior courtyard (bottom)

Interior with courtyards

JB-House [JBH]
Sendai, Miyagi Prefecture, Japan, 2003

In secondary school, the future owner and the architect of this house played soccer together. But at the time they had no idea how significant the game would become later on in their respective lives. While one turned into a professional coach, the other went on to design a 49,000-seat stadium for the World Cup. Though enduring enthusiasm for the sport was not a requirement for winning this house design commission, the coach naturally turned to his former teammate when the time came to build a home of his own.

Married with kids, the client was keen to settle down. Yet finding a desirable property in central Sendai took considerable searching. With Abe's help, he eventually purchased a modest 266 m² (2,863 sq ft) parcel amid a quiet residential enclave not far from the city's commercial hub. Facing a narrow road, the lot looks out towards the picturesque Hirose River in the distance, but a 10-storey apartment tower looms directly behind, compromising the client's privacy.

Faced with these conditions, Abe's primary goal was to simultaneously maximize the view out front and block the sight lines from the building at the back. Instead of adding the individual programmatic pieces together, he decided this project called for an entirely different design strategy. His first move was to create a solid rectilinear box generated from a 3 x 4 grid of nearly square modules. Next, he articulated distinct functional areas by excising rectangular chunks from this conceptual volume that almost completely filled the oblong site. The result was a three-dimensional chessboard of indoor and outdoor rooms that comprise this two-storey 194 m² (2,088 sq ft) house.

Because the client requested covered parking for two cars, the block's front corners were among the first bits to go. These symmetrical niches flank an outdoor entry vestibule and the front door leading into the cross-shaped ground floor. The plan's four wings contain the foyer at the front, the bedroom at the back and the bathroom and study off to either side. For privacy protection, the bedroom's end wall is solid but floor-to-ceiling glass side walls let in plenty of fresh air and daylight. Similarly the study is also enclosed with a single solid and two transparent walls. Made of sliding glass panels, this pair turns the room into a second circulation conduit leading directly from the car park to the terraces and backyard at the rear of the house – a handy feature for a family that enjoys outdoor entertaining.

Upstairs, the floor plan outlines the footprint of the original rectangular block, but is riddled with outdoor spaces. Stretching across the entire front of the house, a large living room opens onto the kitchen on one side and a guest room on the other. These rooms, in turn, connect to two semi-enclosed terraces divided by an interior corridor that joins the front and back of the house where two children's bedrooms and a TV lounge fill out the floor. Though full-height glass links the bedrooms to the terraces, solid walls define their outer corners and shield these private quarters. In the living room, however, Abe wanted to make the river view as accessible as possible, so he took the opposite approach by wrapping both exterior corners with glass. Within the house Abe's extensive transparency yielded a layering of light interior rooms that may be combined in myriad ways by simply pushing partitions aside. In a way, the entire first floor is one room.

In part, the house's composition was made possible by its steel-frame system. Arranged in a 3 x 3.6 m (12 x 12 ft) grid, the frame enabled Abe to separate structure from enclosure and render walls with transparent glass or opaque metal siding at will. Its versatility also gave Abe the freedom to replace columns with cantilevered beams, 7.2 m (24 ft) in one direction and 3 m (10 ft) in the other, which keep the car parks and covered terraces downstairs free of vertical elements. Within the house he concealed the steel members with white painted drywall and blonde maple flooring.

Though Abe did his best to modulate visibility in and out of the house, there was nothing he could do to control the surrounding environment. In a worst-case scenario a building could go up on the lot across the street, severing the connection to the water beyond. 'But even if the view towards the river gets blocked, there is always the view to the sky,' says Abe.

View from the street

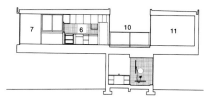

Section

First-floor plan

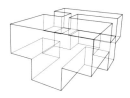

Conceptual diagrams

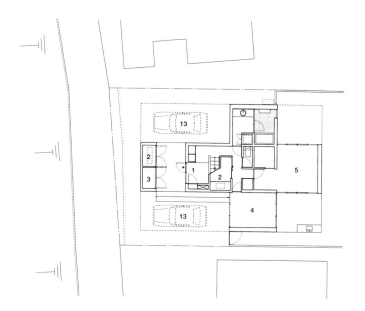

Ground-floor plan

1	Entrance	8	Living room
2	Storage	9	Guest room
3	Mechanical room	10	Terrace
4	Study room	11	Child's bedroom
5	Main bedroom	12	Child's space
6	Kitchen	13	Garage
7	Dining room		

Front facade (top), rear facade (bottom)

JB-House

Stairs to first floor

View from children's space (top), living room (bottom)

K-House [KH]
Sendai, Miyagi Prefecture, Japan, 2002

In Japan, where land values are high and lots are small, big houses on spacious plots are relatively rare. Even in regional cities like Sendai. Completed in 2002, K-House is one of those exceptions. Large by Japanese standards, the 261 m² (2,809 sq ft) home fronts a narrow but busy street amid a residential neighbourhood in the city centre. Composed of two wings, one parallel to the road and the other perpendicular, the cross-shaped building divides the square 496 m² (5,339 sq ft) site into quadrants, each one independent and distinct in character.

In addition to its generous size, the site was essentially free from external constraints, such as immediate neighbours and unsightly adjacencies, which often plague urban sites in Japan. But the clients – a dentist, his wife and their three children – had a number of requests that limited both the relationship of the building to its site and its internal organization.

For starters, the clients wanted to incorporate rental parking spaces into their property – in Japan even the tiniest bits of land can become income-producing assets, since off-street parking is required of all vehicle owners. Yet the family did not want to see or be seen from the parking lot. In fact, they did not want visual contact with the street at all.

Abe's response to these concerns was to front the house with a windowless, concrete wall that cuts clean across the site and completely severs the inner workings of the home from the goings-on outside. Extending out to the street, a second, L-shaped concrete wall subdivides the exposed strip of land into the family carport on one side and six black-topped parking spots on the other. Solid and impenetrable, this barrier simultaneously turns its back on the public rental lot and encloses an alcove open to the house's private forecourt. Capped by a glass canopy, the shielded space serves as bicycle storage and a covered approach to the front door.

Across the threshold, the narrow walkway turns into the entry foyer marking the intersection of the house's two wings. Stretching to the back of the property, the east–west wing holds three bedrooms, a lavatory, storage and the master bedroom on the first floor, and the living room below. Flanked by gardens on either side, the 3.18 m (10 ft) high living room is a hybrid space consisting of a wood-floored, Western-style sitting area followed by a Japanese-style guest room that may be partitioned with sliding *shoji* screens. Made of milky white paper, the screens slip silently across the room, turning the tatami-floored portion into a self-contained box. Upstairs, two circulation spines – one an interior corridor connected to the stairs from below and the other a shallow balcony – straddle the children's bedrooms, each one with its own cosy, built-in sleeping loft at one end and floor-to-ceiling sliding glass doors at the other.

The north–south wing contains a string of functional components that starts with a two-car garage followed by the foyer, stairway and kitchen, a compact cluster of spaces occupying the core of the house. The dining area and bath suite, a trio of independent spaces for soaking, washing and toileting, come next. Defined by counter-height walls on two sides, the kitchen opens to both the living and dining room. 'I like to stand in the kitchen and survey the scenery,' explains the client. Together these three rooms form a continuous, loft-like space oriented towards the large garden that fills the site's southern quadrant.

In contrast to the solid street facade, the back of the house is almost completely transparent and open to the two yards, each one dotted with trees and covered with a mixture of grass and paving stones. Though a perimeter concrete wall unifies the rear of the site and shuts out the surrounding buildings, the gardens are completely separated by the living room – it is necessary to go through the building to get from one outdoor quadrant to another.

Yet architecture and landscape are closely connected by Abe's extensive use of glass, especially in the living room, where expansive fixed panes look north and sliding glass panels face south. Like traditional screens, the panels may be pushed aside, rendering the boundary between interior and exterior practically invisible.

This wide, column-free opening was made possible by the building's steel-frame structural system and Vierendeel truss that eliminated the need for intermediary columns. A rigid box composed of vertical and horizontal steel bars, the truss spans the length of the living room and transfers its load to the solid concrete wall concealed behind the tradition-inspired *tokonoma* display alcove at the far end of the room.

To soften the sharp edges and cold surfaces of the glass, steel and exposed concrete, Abe used warm wood floors, sashes and wall panels on the ground floor. And upstairs, in the bedrooms, white-painted walls and ceilings are washed in sunlight that streams in through the south-facing windows.

But outside Abe assigned materials the important role of distinguishing one building volume from the other. While smooth concrete defines the single-storey block, the two-storey block is clad with striated metal spandrel panels and a textured tile facade. Additional articulation comes from a thin strip of glass inserted between the two blocks. This transparent band not only separates top and bottom – it makes the upper block appear to hover above the lower.

While K-House's blank facade coupled with side windows set back from the street is reminiscent of the Sekii Ladies Clinic, the cross-shaped plan resembles that of M-House. When married to the project's particular conditions, however, the result is not only fresh and new. It enabled Abe to elegantly incorporate mundane parking requirements into a gracious, refined home without compromising privacy or aesthetics.

North facade

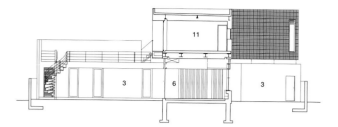

Section

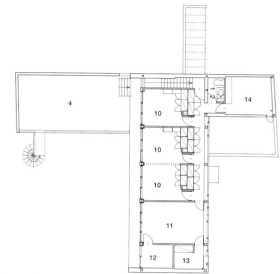

First-floor plan

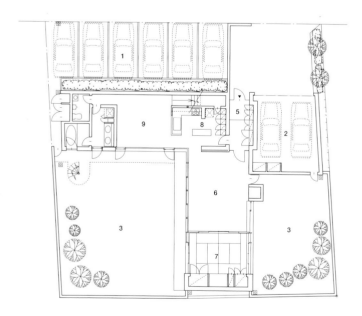

Ground-floor plan

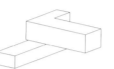

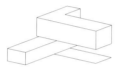

Conceptual diagrams

1	Parking	8	Kitchen
2	Garage	9	Dining room
3	Garden	10	Children's bedrooms
4	Deck	11	Main bedroom
5	Entrance	12	Study room
6	Living	13	Closet
7	Japanese-style room	14	Storage

0   5

Rental parking (top), first-floor terrace (bottom)

K-House Garden (top), dining area (bottom)

First-floor corridor (top), living room (bottom)

Kanno Museum [SSM]
Shiogama, Miyagi Prefecture, Japan, 2005

A metal box for metal sculptures, the Kanno Museum contains a conglomeration of small galleries inspired by soap bubbles but made of pure steel. The brainchild of an art-loving, 70-something psychiatrist eager to share her collection, the museum showcases eight figurative works by Western artists such as Auguste Rodin and Henry Moore. But for Abe it was a chance to try his hand at an entirely unprecedented volumetric compositional method. 'I am more interested in space created by the relationship between people or objects than some kind of abstract system,' says the designer. With that goal in mind, he used the artworks themselves to generate the building's internal cellular structure.

Adjacent to the doctor's palatial home in the Sendai suburb of Shiogama, Abe's Cor-Ten cube bears no resemblance to this or any other house nearby. Its hillside site marks the end of a narrow, circuitous road lined with single-family homes, small apartment buildings and sporadic rice paddies. But Abe's 219 m² (2,370 sq ft) museum is residential in scale only. Set away from the street, the rust-coloured object sits on a concrete pedestal cushioned by lush green grass that physically separates and further distinguishes it from its surroundings. While discreet stairs descend to the client's home west of the site, concrete risers ascend from the museum's parking area to its main entrance, marked with an L-shaped canopy on its east side.

Leaving the mundane street scene behind, the door leads into the reception area but opens onto a magical white world where floors become walls, walls become ceilings and art becomes the focus. Delicate stairs of steel plate descend immediately to the first in a spiralling sequence of irregularly shaped galleries spread out over three levels. Defined by angled walls and connected by slashed openings, the galleries rotate around a central core but are held in place by the building's rectilinear enclosure. The journey culminates at the bottom of the building where the largest of the galleries, which is intended for small concerts as well as art installations, is located. From there a lift headed back upstairs completes the circulation loop. It deposits visitors in a small vestibule where glass floor panels look back at the galleries below but the eye is drawn to a triangular window across the adjacent reception room. Oriented towards the ocean, this opening is one of the few points of contact between the otherworldly interior and exterior reality.

Intent on fostering an intimate relationship between the eight works and their display space, Abe began by drawing a cellular enclosure around the individual artworks, each one a single continuous surface without discernable horizontal or vertical planes. Essentially he designed boundaries between sculptures. He then piled the cells into a 10 x 12 x 10 m (33 x 39 x 33 ft) cube whose dimensions were determined by the site's maximum permissible building volume. Confining the bubbles not only established adjacencies, it secured an otherwise fragile and unstable organizational system. As the design process progressed, some individual barriers broke down, and the one-to-one correlation between each sculpture and its space evolved into a slightly more flexible arrangement that can accommodate temporary exhibitions as well as present the permanent collection in multiple ways.

Dependent on and defined by each other, the soap bubbles' physical properties were the perfect conceptual model for Abe's galleries. And, like soap bubbles, thin steel plate can act as structure and enclosure at the same time. Finding the ideal way to use the metal, however, required thinking outside the proverbial box. But Abe and his team, which included the structural engineer as well as the shipbuilder who crafted the perforated steel sheet lining the restaurant Aoba-tei, took a mere 15 minutes to devise the museum's unique waffle walls.

Used both inside and out, the walls are composed of two 3.2 mm (0.13 in) thick steel plates covered with a grid of 15 x 9 cm (6 x 3 in) lozenge-shaped embossments. Placed back-to-back, these indentations were welded together, merging the barriers into a double-sided wall. Outside, velvety rust will eventually turn a rich, chocolate brown colour and coat the entire building. Inside some of the walls are finished with matt paint only, showing off their dimpled texture. Others had to be covered with an additional layer of wallboard suitable for hanging art. To unify the space and offset the sculptures, every interior surface, even the floors and ceilings, was painted white.

Building almost entirely with steel simplified the construction in some ways and made it more difficult in others. The greatest challenge was that the steel had to be transported as small panels and welded on-site. Using the doctor's driveway as a staging area for the cranes eliminated the problem of access – narrow streets often make this a serious consideration in Japan. But getting all the pieces to fit together perfectly challenged even the torch-wielding shipbuilders who assembled as well as prefabricated the component pieces.

Miraculously the plates fit together with the precision of folded origami paper – even the funnel-shaped roof designed to collect and deposit rainwater into a built-in downspout on the museum's west side. The task of turning the steel shell into a building belonged to the general contractor, who was responsible for everything from the concrete foundations to the interior finishes and window installation. Intended for ambient light, without compromising the cube's integrity or revealing too much of the surroundings, the openings include a triangular skylight that illuminates the ground level, slash-shaped glass insets and the staff office's strip of operable windows. To highlight the displays there are adjustable track fixtures and, mounted where gallery wall meets gallery wall, linear lighting elements that call attention to the interior's underlying cellular structure.

Shortly after the museum opened, the owner asked Abe to create and install an exhibition about his architecture. Instead of the usual models and drawings, Abe used light and colour to put his building on display. Just by affixing gel films to the exterior glass and dotting the floor with globe fixtures, Abe achieved remarkable results. Each room was awash in a spectrum of reds, violets, greens, blues, oranges or yellows that exaggerated the slanting planes and the patterned steel plates. In addition to highlighting the character of the building, Abe literally cast the artworks in a new light by applying tinted coatings to the individual spotlights directed at each pedestal-mounted piece. This yielded a dramatic role reversal: the eight sculptures became the backdrop for the rainbow-hued installation and the underlying architecture.

In essence, this temporary exhibition treated the sculptures and the space in a similar way, by bathing both with coloured light. But, day-to-day, the two are engaged in more of a dialectical relationship. Highly representational human figures, the eight pieces contrast sharply with the scaleless steel planes and abstract volumes whose components barely relate to the body at all. Yet the tension between these two polarities enriches the gallery experience and enhances both the art and the architecture.

Rear facade

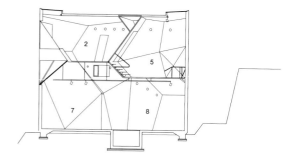

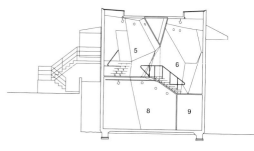

Sections

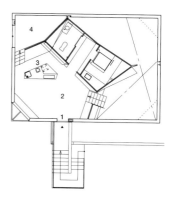

First-floor plan

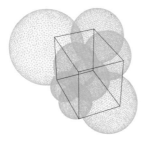

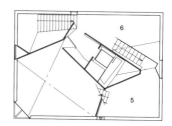

Mezzanine-floor plan

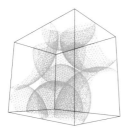

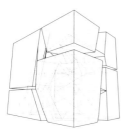

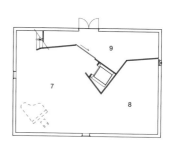

Ground-floor plan

1   Entrance
2   Gallery 1
3   Kitchen
4   Office
5   Gallery 2
6   Gallery 3
7   Gallery 4
8   Gallery 5
9   Storage

Conceptual diagrams

Front facade showing entry sequence, two views

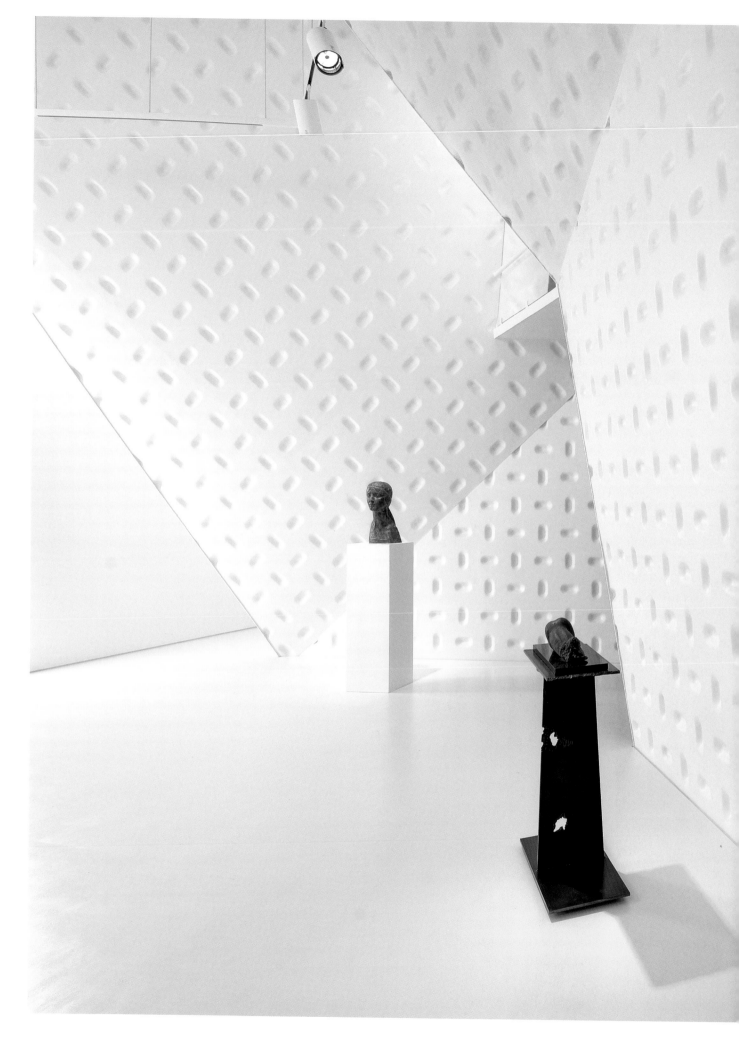

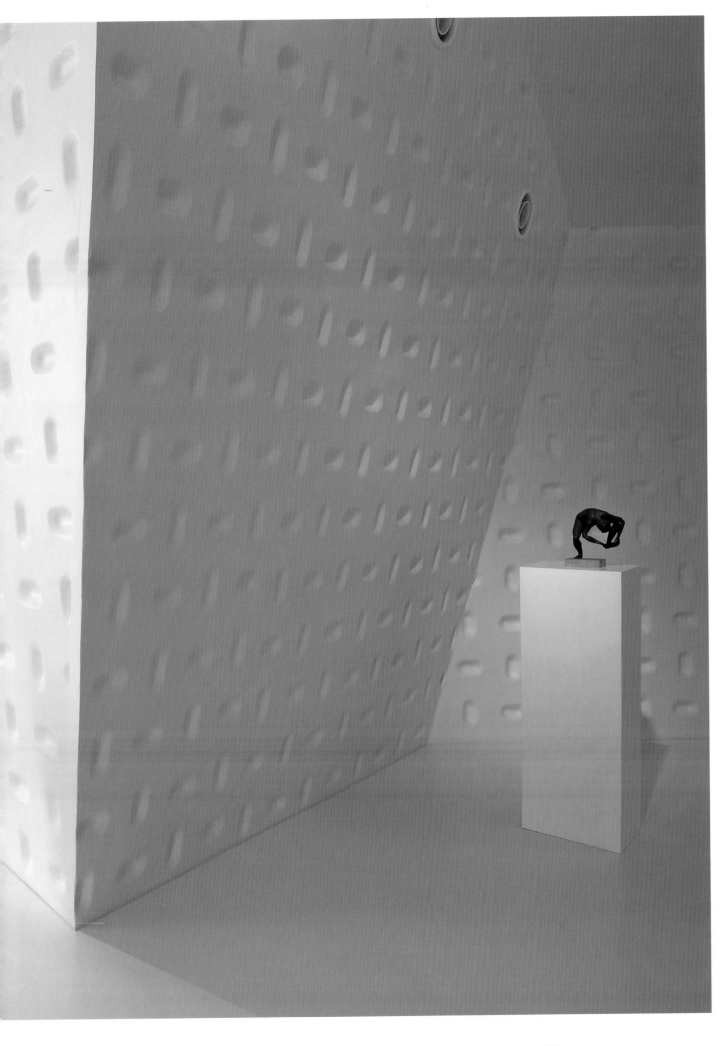

Galleries 4 and 5

Gallery 2

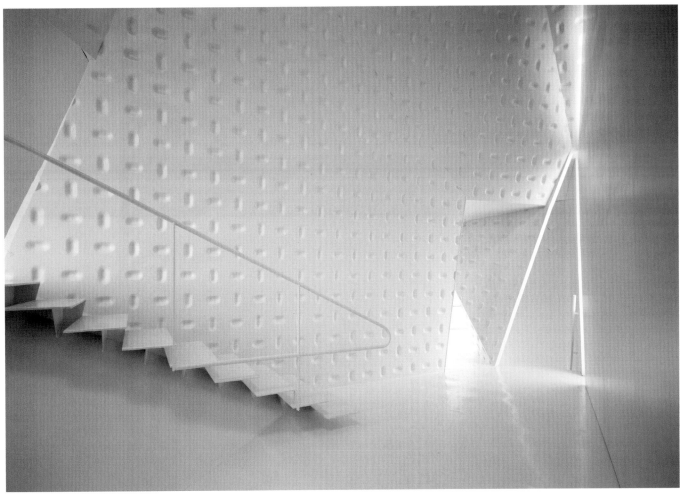

Gallery 1 (top), gallery 2 (bottom)

Whopper [KCH]
Saitama, Saitama Prefecture, Japan, 2006

A combined private residence and paediatric clinic, Whopper is layered like a hamburger but made of concrete, glass and steel. The meat of the 392 m² (4,219 sq ft) building is a patio-wrapped public space for the family that includes the living/dining room and kitchen. Garnished with a few leafy potted plants, it is sandwiched by a 'bun' made of painted white concrete. The top half contains the private quarters and the bottom half the ground-floor clinic.

Stratifying the programme was the idea of the client, a solo practitioner with young children of his own. But the solid–void–solid composition came from Abe, who designed Whopper in tandem with Shumai, another combination home and business modelled after a Chinese dumpling. Though never built, Shumai's public portion literally enveloped the private home like a dumpling's doughy wrapper. For Whopper, Abe created a horizontal gradation of public and private zones that enabled him to meld the family's needs with challenging site conditions. Facing a two-lane commercial thoroughfare, the land was perfect for patient access but less than ideal for raising children.

Set back from the road, a parking area for three vehicles buffers the building from the steady stream of cars out front. The paved lot may not be beautiful but it conveniently abuts the building's two entrances: stairs up to the doctor's home define one end of the facade and a recessed doorway to the clinic occupies the other. Though the doctor must go outside to get to work – there is no internal link between home and clinic – his commuting time can't be beaten.

Friendly and non-institutional, the clinic starts with a foyer where street shoes are exchanged for standard-issue indoor slippers. It opens into a cheery, colourful waiting room at the front. The back holds the treatment and consultation rooms. A doughnut-shaped circulation path connects the two halves as it encircles the reception area and other support functions. Throughout the clinic, walls are painted playful shades of yellow, red and green, and Abe-designed furniture, such as the reception desk and an upholstered bench, are finished with rounded corners that echo the building's smooth edges and double as built-in child-safety devices.

Upstairs, the entrance to the doctor's home is set back from the street by an exterior walkway. It leads to a foyer that opens onto a loft-like, L-shaped space containing living and dining areas, followed by the kitchen separated by a high counter. A *shoji*-screened guest room, complete with a *tokonoma* decorative alcove and a futon storage closet, fills out the rectangular plan. The only shuttered space on the first floor (aside from the bathroom and lavatory), this tradition-inspired room is enclosed with movable partitions made of paper. While tatami mat flooring sets the guest room further apart, black tiles unify all other areas, including the surrounding quasi-outdoor space. A vestige of the wrap-around terrace Abe envisioned initially, a second L-shaped band, this one a covered porch reminiscent of a traditional-style *engawa* veranda, is a visual extension of the glass-walled living and dining area. Here, children play and adults sip tea undisturbed. Abe wanted the inhabitants to feel protected but have views to the outside.

While the floor plane unifies functional zones, the ceiling divides them. As in the Yomiuri Media Miyagi Guest House, the rise from a single to a double ceiling height corresponds to the shift from the eating to the sitting area. But it makes this distinction without impeding the flow of space. Capped by an expansive skylight, the double-height living room also links the top and bottom of the house. Ascending from the living room, cherry-stained wood stairs turn into the second floor's balcony-style corridor, physically connecting the two levels. Open on one side to the seating below, the corridor circulates around the two-storey void. It leads first to separate bathrooms and lavatories, followed by the family's communal bedroom (the space will be divided into three rooms when the children get older) and culminates in the doctor's study, where a single window reconnects with the street.

Because of the unfavourable site conditions (Whopper is also tightly hemmed in on three sides by neighbouring buildings), punctures in the perimeter walls on the ground and second floors were limited to a selection of round-cornered openings for light, sharply edged operable casements and an occasional strip window for view. As is often the case in congested Japanese neighbourhoods, Abe had to rely heavily on natural light from above, especially in the doctor's home. In contrast to the mostly solid plane separating the ground and first floors, the roof and second floor are full of holes. In addition to the central skylight, a metal grille clothes-drying deck on the second floor and corner cut-outs let light filter down to the terrace and the two ground-floor entrances beyond that.

Though essentially a giant window, the first floor's glass wrapping is not a major light source since it is shadowed by the second floor overhead, set back from the house perimeter and partially shielded by the outer walls that extend up from below and down from above. The only place light can enter is through the gap in-between. While the bottom wall is made of steel-reinforced concrete articulated with rounded corners and a smooth surface, the top wall is composed of concrete panels mounted on a steel frame. Sharp corners and a scored pattern define its outer surface. From a distance, the tripartite composition reads as a unified whole, but up close it appears as two separate volumes. This gives it what Abe calls a 'flickering character'.

In contrast to Whopper's rigid exterior shell, the interior is fluid and open. As Abe says, 'This kind of juxtaposition is one way to design an urban house in Japan.' Though this strategy is not without its trade-offs – the house's main spaces are somewhat dark – the family will be ready if a fast-food restaurant sets up shop next door.

Entrance to residence

Street facade

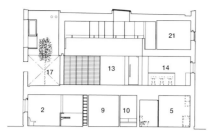

Section

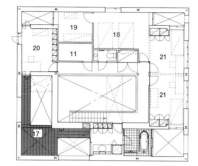

Second-floor plan

First-floor plan

Ground-floor plan

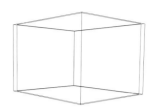

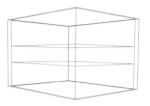

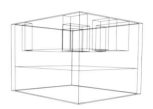

Conceptual diagrams

1	Entrance (clinic)	12	Entrance (residence)
2	Waiting room	13	Living room
3	Isolation room	14	Dining room
4	Medical examination room	15	Kitchen
5	Treatment room	16	Japanese-style room
6	X-ray room	17	Terrace
7	Isolation waiting room	18	Main bedroom
8	Backroom	19	Closet
9	Medical preparation room	20	Study room
10	Breast-feeding room	21	Children's bedroom
11	Storage		

Living room (top left), second-floor terrace (top right),
first-floor covered porch (bottom)

F-town [FRP]
Sendai, Miyagi Prefecture, Japan, 2007

Commonly found on warehouses and other low-cost structures, autoclaved lightweight concrete (ALC) panels are not normally an architect's material of choice. But at F-town, a seven-storey eat-and-drink building filled with bars and restaurants, the mundane material has never looked so good. Located on a busy street amid Sendai's emergent entertainment district, east of the city's main train station, the building was a chance for Abe to transform an inexpensive exterior cladding into intricately carved facades rich with relief. Composed of ALC-covered cubes, Abe's pure white exterior comes to life when the sun rises and casts shadows that bring out its mesmerizing, geometric motifs. Unlike typical bar buildings bedecked with nondescript exterior finishes, F-town does not need signage to stand out. Instead, its textured surfaces and conspicuous absence of colour draw attention day and night.

This wall treatment was another collaboration with the graphic designer Asao Tokolo, who worked with Abe on the facades of the pachinko parlours PTI and PTK. Here they devised two 25 cm (10 inch) square, patterned units – one features circles and the other crosses – and used them to disguise the concrete panels' ungainly 4 m (13 ft) by 60 cm (2 ft) dimensions. Produced with a digital milling machine, their carved lines just graze the top layer of each 12 cm (5 in) thick panel, but the sculpted boxes read as individually cast tiles. At the same time, the panels' large size had the advantage of minimizing distracting grout lines, which contributes to the building's remarkably consistent exterior wrapping.

On close inspection, however, the building's facades are actually all different. Though three are clad with the ALC panels (the fourth, which practically touches its neighbour and conceals the base building's lift and stairs, was simply coated with grey paint), each one varies volumetrically, since the building exterior is an assemblage of six stacked cubes, not flat walls. Balanced on top of each other, the boxes, each one completely clad with one of the two types of patterned ALC panels, jut out in different directions. In addition, void spaces concentrated in the building's outer corners physically separate one protrusion from the next.

In part, the two-storey cubes were a means of creating a highly articulated building mass that has a distinctive appearance and maximizes the site's permissible volume. But Abe also wanted to derive a new solution to the standard Japanese restaurant tower: formulaic floor upon floor of sushi counters, wine bars and pizza parlours accessed independently from street level. Whereas usually such buildings depend on lifts and one does not experience a connection between levels, Abe provided more options. He set up the possibility of the double-height volumes expressed on the building exterior and created the infrastructure for an additional circulatory system that could connect each tenant space to its neighbours.

By installing stairs in the void spaces between boxes, tenants of the building can create two-storey shops of their own or connect directly to someone else above or below. 'I tried to plant the possibility of an urban relationship between the restaurants in the building,' explains the architect. If every restaurateur buys into this scheme, an additional, spiral-shaped loop could develop around the building perimeter, enabling bar-hopping customers to move easily from place to place.

But this will take some doing, since the tenants are responsible for their own interiors and may not follow through with the ideas suggested by Abe's base building design. Taking this into account, Abe divided the interior into single-storey, L-shaped levels (not the two-storey boxes shown outside). Each one is sandwiched between 45 cm (18 inch) thick floors with plenty of room for plumbing pipes and ventilation ducts. Free from the usual stacked kitchens and bathrooms, tenants are able to place fixtures and appliances where desired without intruding on the adjacent spaces.

Due to varying ceiling heights and void spaces, the character and street exposure at each floor is different. But the base building amenities – lifts and two sets of egress stairs bound by aluminium-panelled corridors – are constant, top to bottom. Every floor is accessed from the street-level lobby where entrances lead in from two sides of the building. Occupying a corner site bounded by streets on two sides, the new building is well positioned. It is not only a block from Miyagino Street, a newly widened thoroughfare leading from Sendai Station to the Rakuten Golden Eagles baseball stadium 2 km (10 miles) away; it also sits on top of the new subway line that will be up and running in 2015. With a location like this and its striking appearance, F-town has what it takes to become a landmark destination.

South facade

Seventh-floor plan

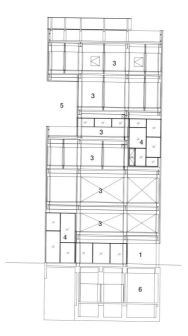

Section

Third-floor plan

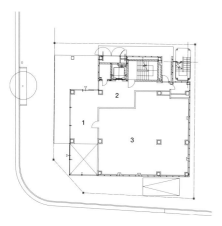

Ground-floor plan

1   Main entrance
2   Lift shaft
3   Tenant space
4   Void
5   Terrace
6   Mechanical room

Conceptual diagrams

0   5

Spiralling cubic volumes

F-town

South and east facades

Exterior wall detail (top left), tenant space (top right),
view from street (bottom)

Index

Italic numbers refer to illustrations

Project Credits

MSP/Miyagi Stadium
Rifu, Miyagi-gun, Miyagi Prefecture
1994–2000
Project Architect: Hitoshi Abe, Katsunori Abe, Hideo Yaguchi, Yoshikatsu Matsuno
Collaborator: Shoichi Haryu Architect & Associates
Structural Engineer: Kozo Keikaku Kenkyujyo, Koken Gijyutu Consultant
M&E Engineer: Sogo Consultants, Tohoku
Contractor: Kajima JV, Niitsuma JV, Asahi JV, Yuatech JV

SBP/Shirasagi Bridge
Shiroishi, Miyagi Prefecture
1993–1994
Project Architect: Hitoshi Abe, Yoshikatsu Matsuno, Hideo Yaguchi
Structural Engineer: Asia Kousoku
Contractor: Zenitaka Corporation

MRP/Neige Lune Fleur
Aoba-ku, Sendai, Miyagi Prefecture
1999
Project Architect: Hitoshi Abe, Hideo Yaguchi
M&E Engineer: Sogo Consultants, Tohoku
Contractor: Alcoa

MYH/Matsushima Yacht House
Matsushima, Miyagi Prefecture
1998–2000
Project Architect: Hitoshi Abe, Hideo Yaguchi, Katsunori Abe, Takemi Watanabe
Structural Engineer: TIS & Partners
M&E Engineer: Sogo Consultants, Tohoku
Contractor: Ito Koumuten

NH/N-House
Kamakura, Kanagawa Prefecture
1999–2000
Project Architect: Hitoshi Abe, Hideo Yaguchi
Structural Engineer: TIS & Partners
M&E Engineer: Sogo Consultants, Tohoku
Contractor: Inoue Kogyo

IH/I-House
Taihaku-ku, Sendai, Miyagi Prefecture
2000–2001
Project Architect: Hitoshi Abe, Naoki Inada
Structural Architect: NS Sekkei
M&E Engineer: Sogo Consultants, Tohoku
Contractor: Nikken Kensetsu Kogyo

KAP/Reihoku Community Hall
Reihoku, Amakusa-gun, Kumamoto
Prefecture
2000–2003
Project Architect: Hitoshi Abe,
Hideo Yaguchi, Naoto Misawa
Collaborator: Yasuaki Onoda (Tohoku
University)
Structural Engineer: TIS & Partners
M&E Engineer: Sogo Consultants,
Tohoku
Contractor: Nakamura Corporation +
Kanematsu JV

MWT/Miyagi Water Tower
Rifu, Miyagi-gun, Miyagi Prefecture
1993–1994
Project Architect: Hitoshi Abe, Hideo
Yaguchi, Hirotoki Abe, Naoki Inada
Collaborator: Shoichi Haryu Architect
& Associates
Structural Engineer: SDG
M&E Engineer: Sogo Consultants,
Tohoku
Contractor: Miyagi Construction

**YG/Yomiuri Media Miyagi Guest
House**
Zao, Katta-gun, Miyagi Prefecture
1995–1997
Project Architect: Hitoshi Abe,
Yoshikatsu Matsuno, Hideo Yaguchi,
Hideyuki Mori
Structural Engineer: TIS & Partners
M&E Engineer: Sogo Consultants,
Tohoku
Contractor: Sugawara Construction +
Nihon Jutaku Eizen

KIR/Michinoku Folklore Museum
Kurihara, Miyagi Prefecture
1998–2000
Project Architect: Hitoshi Abe,
Naoki Inada, Takayuki Saitou
Structural Engineer: NS Sekkei +
Junichi Onose (Tohoku Institute
of Technology)
M&E Engineer: Sogo Consultants,
Tohoku
Contractor: Miyagi Construction

**SOB/Sasaki Office Factory for
Prosthetics**
Aoba-ku, Sendai, Miyagi Prefecture
2002–2004
Project Architect: Hitoshi Abe,
Hideo Yaguchi, Naoto Misawa
Structural Engineer: Arup Japan
M&E Engineer: Sogo Consultants,
Tohoku
Contractor: Ando Corporation

AIP/Aoba-tei
Aoba-ku, Sendai, Miyagi Prefecture
2003–2005
Project Architect: Hitoshi Abe,

Hideo Yaguchi, Naoki Inada,
Yasuyuki Sakuma
Structural Engineer: Arup Japan
M&E Engineer: Sogo Consultants,
Tohoku
Lighting Design: Masahide Kakudate
Lighting Architect & Associates, Inc.
Contractor: Hokushin Koei,
Takahashi Kogyo (steel panel)

NHB/Tokyo House KADO 001
Shibuya-ku, Tokyo
2004–2005
Project Architect: Hitoshi Abe,
Katsunori Abe, Masatoshi Tobe
Collaborator: Commdesign
(producer)
Structural Engineer: Oak Structural
Design
M&E Engineer: Sogo Consultants,
Tohoku
Lighting Design: Masahide Kakudate
Lighting Architect & Associates, Inc.
Contractor: Hino Kensetsu

TH9/9 Tsubo House TALL
Chigasaki, Kanagawa Prefecture
2004–2005
Project Architect: Hitoshi Abe,
Naoki Inada, Noriko Rinno
Structural Engineer: Oak Structural
Design
M&E Engineer: Sogo Consultants,
Tohoku
Contractor: Tosho Corporation

PTI/Pachinko Tiger Izumi Matsumori
Izumi-ku, Sendai, Miyagi Prefecture
2003
Project Architect: Hitoshi Abe,
Hideo Yaguchi, Naoki Inada,
Takayuki Saito
Collaborator: Asao Tokolo (facade
design)
Structural Engineer: Arup Japan
M&E Engineer: Arup Japan
Contractor: Fujita Corporation,
Tohoku

PTK/Pachinko Tiger Kagitori
Taihakuku-ku, Sendai, Miyagi
Prefecture
2004–2005
Project Architect: Hitoshi Abe,
Hideo Yaguchi, Azuma Orikasa
Collaborator: Asao Tokolo (facade
design)
Structural Engineer: Arup Japan
M&E Engineer: Arup Japan
Contractor: Konoike Construction
Co., Ltd

DIP/Dining Dayu
Aoba-ku, Sendai, Miyagi Prefecture
2003
Project Architect: Hitoshi Abe,

Hideo Yaguchi, Naoto Misawa
M&E Engineer: Sogo Consultants,
Tohoku
Contractor: Ishiguro Architectural
Design Workshop

G2P/Gravel 2
Aoba-ku, Sendai, Miyagi Prefecture
1996–1998
Project Architect: Hitoshi Abe,
Naoki Inada
Structural Engineer: TIS & Partners
M&E Engineer: Sogo Consultants,
Tohoku
Contrctor: Nihon Jyutaku Eizen

MH/M-House
Haramachi, Minamisouma,
Fukushima Prefecture
1998–1999
Project Architect: Hitoshi Abe,
Naoki Inada, Takmi Watanabe
Structural Engineer: Junichi Onose
(Tohoku Institute of Tecnology)
Contractor: Nishiuchi Koumuten

ADC/M-Dental Clinic
Aoba-ku, Sendai, Miyagi Prefecture
2000–2001
Project Architect: Hitoshi Abe,
Naoki Inada
Structural Engineer: Structured
Environment
M&E Engineer: Sogo Consultants,
Tohoku
Contractor: Takaya Corporation

FLC/Sekii Ladies Clinic
Osaki, Miyagi Prefecture
2000–2001
Project Architect: Hitoshi Abe,
Katsunori Abe, Takayuki Saito,
Noriko Rinno
Structural Engineer: TIS & Partners
M&E Engineer: Sogo Consultants,
Tohoku
Contractor: Takaya Corporation

YH/Y-House
Yamagata, Yamagata Prefecture
2001–2003
Project Architect: Hitoshi Abe,
Katsunori Abe, Naoki Inada,
Noriko Rinno, Takayuki Saitou
Structural Engineer: Oak Structural
Design
M&E Engineer: Sogo Consultants,
Tohoku
Contractor: Nikken Kensetsu Kogyo

JBH/JB-House
Wakabayashi-ku ,Sendai, Miyagi
Prefecture
2002–2003
Project Architect: Hitoshi Abe,
Naoki Inada, Kazuya Saitou

Structural Engineer: Oak Structural
Design
M&E Engineer: Sogo Consultants,
Tohoku
Contractor: Ito Koumuten

KH/K-House
Aoba-ku, Sendai, Miyagi Prefecture
2001–2002
Project Architect: Hitoshi Abe,
Katsunori Abe, Naoto Misawa
Structural Engineer: Oak Structural
Design
M&E Engineer: Sogo Consultants,
Tohoku
Contractor: Nikken Kensetsu Kogyo

SSM/Kanno Museum
Shiogama, Miyagi Prefecture
2003–2005
Project Architect: Hitoshi Abe,
Katsunori Abe, Takuma Ishikawa
Structural Engineer: Oak Structural
Design
M&E Engineer: Sogo Consultants,
Tohoku
Contractor: Kajima Corporation,
Takahashi Kogyo

KCH/Whopper
Saitama, Saitama Prefecture
2004–2006
Project Architect: Hitoshi Abe,
Katsunori Abe, Takuma Ishikawa,
Naoto Misawa
Structural Engineer: TIS & Partners
M&E Engineer: Sogo Consultants,
Tohoku
Lighting Design: Masahide Kakudate
Lighting Architect & Associates, Inc.
Contractor: Fujita, Kanto

FRP/F-town
Miyagino-ku, Sendai, Miyagi
Prefecture
2003–2007
Project Architect: Hitoshi Abe,
Hideo Yaguchi, Takayuki Saito,
Azuma Orikasa
Collaborator: Asao Tokolo (facade
design)
Structural Engineer: Arup Japan
M&E Engineer: Sogo Consultants,
Tohoku
Contractor: Iwata Chisaki Inc,
Tohoku

Phaidon Press Limited
Regent's Wharf
All Saints Street
London N1 9PA

Phaidon Press Inc.
180 Varick Street
New York, NY 10014

www.phaidon.com

First published 2008
© 2008 Phaidon Press Limited

ISBN 978 0 7148 4665 1

A CIP catalogue record for this book is available from
the British Library.

Designed by Joost Grootens
Printed in China

Front and back cover: Kanno Museum and Reihoku
Community Hall. Photographs by Daici Ano.

Author's acknowledgements
I would like to extend my heartfelt thanks to Hitoshi Abe.
Without Hitoshi's commitment and full participation, this
book would not have been possible. I am very grateful to
Tohru Horiguchi of Tohoku University who provided valuable
input and a variety of assistance all along the way. I would
also like to thank Karen Stein for launching this project
and Emilia Terragni for seeing it through to completion.
In addition, I wish to thank Alexa Kempton and Cameron
Laux for their superb editorial skills.

I am especially appreciative of my family's steady
encouragement and enthusiastic embrace of this project.
I am delighted to dedicate this book to Abby, Eve and David.

Note
Each project is identified by its formal name and, where
applicable, the abbreviated title assigned by the
architect-in-charge. The acronyms are compilations of letters
taken from the programme, location or the client's name.

Picture credits

Numbers indicate page number.
t=top, b=bottom, l=left, c=centre, r=right

Daici Ano: 1, 15, 18, 19, 20(b), 63(b), 65, 66, 69(tr), 70, 71(t, bl),
101, 103, 106(t), 109, 117, 119(b), 120, 122, 123(b), 129(t), 131,
133(t), 134, 135, 137, 139, 140, 145, 157, 159, 161(tl), 163, 165,
166(t), 167, 169, 171, 172, 175, 177, 178, 179, 181, 183(b), 185,
189(b), 192, 193, 195, 196, 199, 203, 204, 205(tl, b)
Atelier Hitoshi Abe: 7, 8, 11, 12, 14(t, c), 16, 23, 37, 75, 143
Shunichi Atsumi: 14(b), 27, 31(b), 32, 34(b), 39(b), 40, 43,
45(tr), 47, 49, 50, 87, 88, 90(b), 93, 95, 97(b), 98, 166(b)
commdesign inc.: 125
Eiji Kitada: 28, 33(b)
Narihara Architecture Photo: 53, 55, 56(t), 57(tr)
Sergio Pirrone: 113(t), 114, 190
Katsuaki Sato: 133(b)
Shinkenchiku-sha: 9, 10, 17, 20(t, c), 25, 31(t), 33(t), 34(t), 35,
39(t), 45(tl, b), 51, 56(b), 57(tl, b), 59, 61, 62, 63(t), 69(tl), 71(br),
77, 79, 81, 82, 83, 90(t), 91, 96, 97(t), 104, 106(b), 107, 110,
111, 113(b), 119(t), 123(t), 127, 128, 129(b), 150, 151, 153, 155,
160, 161(tr, b), 183(t), 184, 187, 189(t), 201, 205(tr)
Shokokusha Photographers: 69(b), 85
Yoshimori Yaegashi: 147, 149
Chiaki Yasukawa: 72